Scholarship, Leadership, & Service
The Evolution of a High School Black Student Union

Scholarship, Leadership, & Service
The Evolution of a High School Black Student Union

Kenneth L. Turner

Kenneth L. Turner

Scholarship, Leadership, & Service by Kenneth L. Turner

Printed in the United States of America
First Printing, 2022

Paperback Book ISBN: 9798831818420
Imprint: Independently published

To Mama,
your love and belief in me
have always been the ultimate affirmation.

To Daddy,
you were the caring man in the life of a child
that I continue to aspire to be. Thank you for your
presence.

Table of Contents

Kenneth L. Turner

Preface

High school is as much a social experience as it is an educational one. If that were not clear before Covid, it certainly should be now. The thought that children are in school to get an education reminds me of what I used to tell my Math students when they tried to solve equations. It's right, but it's not complete. Children are in school to get an education, but they are also there to learn how to function in a society, to learn how to navigate relationships, and to be able to identify and connect with people of similar interests, and also to be able to identify unhealthy relationships for that matter. We are social beings and when we did not have that social interaction it had a devastating effect on children and adults alike. Quite often just being at school is not enough though. Students sometimes need a deeper connection to their peers. Adults do too. Attending college may not be enough so we join fraternities and sororities, or other student organizations. We may want more of a connection to our job so we join professional associations. We may choose to join social clubs to feel more of a sense of belonging. Children are no different. When they are at school, just going to class and going home may not be sufficient. While they do have the human interaction, it may not equate to that same sense of belonging. Some have the athletic ability or interest so they join teams. They may have the talent or the desire to learn music, and so they join the band. They find programs that are offered at the school that align with their interests and they join voluntarily, at least in most cases, because that is where their interest and/or passion lies. The same is true of clubs. On any high school campus there may be dozens of clubs and organizations. At Hamilton High School, where I have worked for the past 15 years, there is usually at least 50 such clubs ranging from all types of interests. There are community service clubs for those who have a particular interest in serving others. There are hobby clubs for students who have more specific interests. There are ethnic identity clubs for students of similar backgrounds who want to bond over issues that affect their community. All these clubs, or affinity groups, have one thing in common. They are voluntary. Students join because they want to. There is no club that is mandated to be on a campus. They are all optional, and since they are optional, what each club does is also optional. There are rules that govern a club's activities, but within those guidelines, how much or how little a club (or club sponsor), does is totally up to that club. When it comes to creating a positive experience for students on a high school campus, clubs can be just the solution. And when it comes to creating a positive experience for Black students particularly, the Black Student Union is one such club that has proven to positively impact the school community, and have a positive influence on its members. But first, you have to reimagine the way you see clubs on a high school campus.

Clubs on a high school campus are usually the idea of a student or group of students because they have a particular interest or cause. They then seek out a faculty member who they think would support their idea and ask if that faculty member would like to be the sponsor of their club. At that moment, the faculty member can choose to accept or deny the request and decide how much time or involvement they choose to give to the club. In my experience, what usually happens, if the faculty member says yes, they take a very limited role in the club's activities and an even lesser role in meetings. It usually comes down to signing the club application so the club can happen in the first place, and then the school may never know who the sponsor is, much less see them with the club. Now while it is true that these are student-led organizations and the students are much more visible, who guides the students if the sponsor takes such a limited role? Moreover, what happens when the school year ends if the leaders are seniors? Even if the leaders are freshmen, does the club continue after their four-year run? These are just questions of consistency, but what about impact? How will the club impact the school community? What kind of influence will the club have on the members of the club? I suggest that in order to have a consistently stable, and even consistently growing club, that has a positive impact on a school culture and community, and has a positive influence on its members, it is essential that the sponsor play a major role in all aspects of the club, all year. That means that it can't be just another club. The sponsor must see the club as another job on campus. Now here comes the tough sell. It's an *unpaid* job. It will require much time, which will take time from other parts of the job, and even your personal life. It will require lots of support from your administration, who will hopefully see the value in what you are doing for the students and the entire school community. The sponsor must either have, or be able to build strong relationships with the students, all the students. Building relationships with your own members gives the club a central figure and a more solid foundation. Building relationships with all the students gives your club credibility, respect, and a good reputation overall. How do you build these relationships with students? I believe you do it the same way you build relationships with adults. It takes time, which many educators do not have. As you build trust with the students they will want, and need, to talk to you about situations they face, both in and out of school. They will come to you for wisdom, for guidance, for comfort, for reassurance, and for affirmation. This can be many students, not just a few. You will want to be there for all of them. This is why our disposition is so important. We must always be in the space to help a student because we never know when we will be needed. Not all of your students will need that all the time, but any one of them could need that at any given time. Sometimes the right word, or the answer to a question might be needed as you are simply walking to the restroom and one of your students sees you, and needs a quick minute. You could be walking to your car to go home after a long day. It doesn't have to always be lengthy conversations, but students need to know that you are walking this high school journey with them. This happens when you are consistently there with the right disposition. Sometimes you might have to tell them what they don't want to hear, but they will accept it as long as they know it's coming from a place of love.

This book is for anyone who is looking for a place and an opportunity to have a positive influence on students, in this case Black students. I want you to know that you can do this, but it is going to require a lot. It may not look the same as it does at Hamilton High School, but the impact and influence can still be the same. If you have the passion and desire to see students succeed, and the time to commit to taking the journey through high school with them, you will find this one of the most rewarding experiences imaginable.

Introduction

This is the story of an amazing group of young people. For the past 15 years I have worked at Alexander Hamilton High School in Los Angeles, California. During this time, I have carried titles such as Teacher, Intervention Coordinator, Restorative Justice Teacher-Advisor, Restorative Justice Coordinator, Athletic Director, Coach, and ASB (Associated Student Body) Sponsor. The one title that I have carried the longest, and the only one in which I do not receive any pay has been by far my favorite part of the job. I am the Black Student Union Advisor, and it is in this role that I have gotten to work with this amazing group of young people, Hamilton High School's BSU.

I became the BSU advisor knowing nothing about how to fulfill this role. There was no job description, no rubric, and no one to ask. From what I had heard and seen, I didn't have to do much, and that was fine with me. That is until I starting meeting with the students. I began to see who they were and the talents they possessed when only a month into my role we had to produce a Black History program for the entire school. There were only a handful of student leaders in this club, but they were also the leaders of the school. They were small but mighty. They were fully aware of the task at hand, and all they needed was someone to sign on as their sponsor so they could put together a show. I didn't know what I was getting into, but neither did they. As we spent time together meeting to plan the show, we were getting to know each other. But when the show was over, the real work began. Now it was time to build a club.

In this book you will see how this amazing group came together, and stayed together. You will see how we continued to build year after year and why so many students have consistently wanted to be a part of the BSU. You will meet the amazing leaders that have advanced the club year after year. Many of these leaders were general members who always had the leadership potential in them. They just waited for their opportunity to hold a position. You will meet incoming freshmen who knew nothing about clubs and dreaded giving up their lunchtime to attend meetings, and then you will meet freshmen who came in having heard about BSU and could not wait to get involved. Then you will see how those same freshmen progressed to become senior leaders. You will see various activities we have on our calendar, and how many more opportunities come out of nowhere. You will be invited into our meetings to see how we discuss certain topics and determine our agenda.

Finally, you will get a chance to see the impact our BSU has had on the Hamilton High School campus culture and its influence on the members of the club. A club that started as a club and then became an organization, then more like a family, and now a full-fledged brand on campus. This is the evolution that our BSU has experienced, and yours can too. This family grew close because of the time spent together, the many conversations, and the commitment to the guiding principles of scholarship, leadership, and service. The way we relate to one another always comes from a disposition to see the other person become the best version of themselves. How can a club have such an impact on a campus community? Clubs are voluntary. Students join because they want to. The question is what is the mission and vision of the club? If students sign up to join a club, and the mission, vision, and direction of the club leads them toward a desired result of academic excellence, or at least improvement, then that is what they have voluntarily signed up for. If the mission is about developing leaders, then that is what they signed up for. If the club is about community service, that again is what they voluntarily signed up for. Now the advisor, and just as importantly, the club leaders must hold all the members accountable. Because of the sense of belonging they experience, they want to be held accountable.

In this book you will come across many names, and it still doesn't include all the names of the members over the last 12 years. Although the leaders are highlighted, they are not the extent of the BSU. It is through the general body that you can see the real impact on the campus as a whole. There are instances in the book where you will see the entire BSU together, and then you will see how they truly impact the campus. Each chapter in the book represents a school year with chapter one being the 2011 school year and so on. Therefore, the students from the early chapters have all finished high school, obviously, and most have finished college and are well into successful careers. Some are even in the public eye. Our recent graduates are making their way through college, and the freshmen of chapter nine are currently seniors. During the span of twelve years as advisor, I have developed great relationships with literally thousands of students. These relationships do not end when they graduate from high school. Our alumni are very important members of the Hamilton BSU family, and whenever they come back to visit, it is a big deal, and we have special BSU meetings for that very purpose. I have enjoyed a great relationship with the BSU parents as well. It is my desire that they have the peace of mind when their children are under my care that someone at school is looking out for them. I take that responsibility very seriously. While it is true that I am closer with some of the students than I am with others, I am accessible to all of them. My goal is that our BSU has a positive influence on every member. From field trips to guest speakers, from the Yard Show to the BSU Show and all the other campus activities, nothing keeps the BSU together more than our weekly meetings when the students open up to one another. Our involvement and participation in the UBSUC (United Black Student Unions of California), has taken our students to another level of leadership that now expands outside of our campus to all three regions of California. This organization has voted us California's BSU of the Year four consecutive years.

There is no club that is mandated to be on a campus. They are all optional, and since they are optional, what each club does is also optional. There are rules that govern a club's activities, but within those guidelines, how much or how little a club does is totally up to that club. We do a lot. We do things that support our aims of scholarship, leadership, and service. We have fun. Each year the leadership changes, but the ideas and the desire to advance the club continues. The pride and ownership of the family remains strong. What started with about 20 students has grown to as many as over 500. They realize they have something that's bigger than themselves. It's bigger than me. It is bigger than all of us. We graciously invite you into our safe space.

The Club

1
More Than a Show

On any normal school day, it doesn't take too long to finish up the day's work, gather my belongings, or anything else I might need to take home for the day, and find my place in the afternoon Los Angeles traffic going home, but on this rather sunny and warm mid-January afternoon I stayed in my classroom a little longer than usual. I had asked my mother to pick up my daughter Kenya from school, (mama loved picking her up), so I didn't have to be in my usual hurry to leave. It was rare that you would find me in my classroom a half-hour after school had dismissed which is why I was surprised to hear a knock on the door around 3:30. Her name was Keara Williams. She had just graduated from Hamilton seven months earlier and now she attended UCLA, but worked in our UCLA After-School office certain days of the week. I got to know Keara during her senior year. We always spoke as she walked past my classroom, always seeming to be taking care of some business, which was confirmed during our short and light conversations. There was something about her that gave the impression that she had transcended high school and was mentally already in college. That is why I was not surprised when she told me that she had gotten accepted into UCLA. Now "my favorite Bruin" as I referred to her was knocking on my door coming to ask me if I would be willing to sponsor the Black Student Union. She shared with me that the students had asked around and no teacher seemed willing to sponsor the club, and that if they couldn't find anyone, then there would not be a BSU. "What do I have to do?" I asked her. I had no idea what a club sponsor does and had not been involved in any extracurricular programs at Hamilton during my first three years there. I was hired as a Special Education teacher in the fall of 2007 after recently graduating from Cal State L.A. with a master's degree in Communication Studies as well as coaching their women's basketball team. I had not been a full-time teacher for a few years but it felt good to be back in the classroom and there were a lot of things I liked about teaching at Hamilton. Keara told me that all I had to do in this role of sponsor was to simply sign the club application as their sponsor and let them use my room to hold their meetings, and pretty much "check in with them," and that was all. Certainly not wanting them to lose the club I agreed to be the sponsor, but there was a small detail that was not discussed that I learned later when I met the club leaders. It was already mid-January and the annual Black History program was scheduled for the end of February. The problem was that there was no plan nor any idea what the show was going to be about. We had approximately 5 weeks to create, audition, write, rehearse, and perform a show that we would all be proud of, and that would represent the excellence that we all believed such a show should display. What had I gotten myself into?

It was my first time meeting the leadership of the BSU, but it was not my first time seeing them. I knew they were leaders because many of them were also the leaders of the student body in addition to the BSU. The Associated Student Body (ASB) room was right across the hall from my room so I constantly saw the students coming and going during passing periods. These students were clearly the leaders of the school and it wasn't hard to figure that out, and many of them were also close friends. As a Special Education teacher, I had smaller classes and focused all my energy on what I did within my four walls. It was an exciting new challenge for me to be now working with the school leaders. I had no idea how close I would become with them and future leaders.

The BSU President was Portia Amofa, a daughter of African immigrants who was extremely intelligent and also very caring. Portia was all about service to the Hamilton community and she had the utmost respect from her peers and the faculty. She was not only the BSU President but she was also the Student Body President, and what I soon realized was that there was a correlation between BSU leadership and student body leadership. That is why it was so important for the students to find a sponsor. These student leaders did not want to lose this very important club, this very important part of their high school experience. Portia, like Keara the year before, was always about taking care of business, and with her dual roles in school leadership she needed the help of other strong leaders. Selihah White was the BSU Vice

President. She was a strong, very smart, and dedicated student-leader who knew a lot about black history and was good for the club. She gave me the impression that she was her own person and very comfortable with herself. She seemed to me to be a deep thinker who was more concerned with the Black than she was with the union. And then there were the "Bad Girls." These were close friends of Portia who served in the associated student body with her, and by all accounts were her best friends, her crew. Kambria Ruffin, Kiera Johnson, and Breonica Guest-Harding were the three who, along with Portia became known as the Bad Girls. Anything but bad, these were all very respectful, intelligent, and quite funny young ladies. I realized that when I began to frequently meet with them after school. While Portia held the positions of ASB and BSU President, Kiera held the position of Senior Class President, and Kambria served as senior class Treasurer. Breonica was in either ASB, senior class, or both. This group became the body who would take on the task of our first item of business, the BSU show. Also, this would be the first time that the students, in their mind, got to play a major role in the planning of the show. I pledged to lend whatever knowledge and ability I could to make sure the show was a success.

The meetings were held in my room every day after school. The more we talked I began to get a sense of the theme we wanted for the show. They wanted to highlight different eras in black history in America. It seemed easy enough. We simply had to research and find impactful people and events through the decades and portray what we found on stage. Portia gave me the most helpful advice and that was while covering these different eras they didn't want the stories to be "cliché." I learned from these students that whatever they did learn about black history in school was very narrow in scope at best. They wanted to explore and explain parts of black history that neither they, nor their peers studied much, and they were eager to tell those stories. This excited me. We decided that we would do a time travel through certain eras of black history; the question now was how would we tell the story? This is when I began to learn just how much talent existed at our school. The team started recruiting their friends to come to the meetings and before I realized I'm sitting with outstanding singers, dancers, poets, writers, and the most creative young minds that I had ever met. One of the students they recruited stood out to me. He brought a lot of knowledge, maturity, and clarity to what they were trying to produce. His name was

Preston. Preston was not your typical high school student. He had a professionalism about himself that transcended high school. He was a minister. The students saw him as both peer and counselor. He was a major contributor to how the story was told. They settled on the idea that the story would be told on a boat by a hostess who was leading the audience on a trip down the Nile River. Now you may ask what the Nile River has to do with Black History in America, but the idea was much like the ride at Disneyland called It's A Small World. If you have ever been on that boat ride you could see cultures from all over the world as you slowly drift on the water from the beginning to end of the ride. Similarly, at various intervals, the hostess would direct the audience's attention to a particular era, and those would be the different acts and scenes in the show. With all the talent at our disposal we knew that some scenes would feature our dancers, some would be songs, and others would be told or depicted through spoken word. The eras covered would be slavery, the Reconstruction Era, Harlem Renaissance, Civil Rights Movement, and the Black Power movement, and the show would be seventy minutes in length. Kambria was chosen to play the part as hostess/tour guide on this trip we were about to take our audience.

The show was cast and the script was written, both by the BSU leaders, and now it was our time for all-day rehearsal. At our school, each ethnic group had a date set aside to perform an assembly for the entire school. During the show week, we get the day before the show in the auditorium all day for rehearsal. That day was a memorable one. I knew nothing about how these shows had been put together in the past. I knew only a few of the many students who showed up to rehearsal, but I also knew that I was the faculty sponsor and I was in charge, and would ultimately be responsible for not only that day in the auditorium, but for the entire show. My strategy was to meet with the students and gain a clear understanding of what the leaders wanted, and then empower them to lead their peers in this effort. I worked with the students who would be helping back stage, those who would work as ushers, and those who were assigned to control the lights and the sound. I also had the final say of who could participate in the show based on their behavior, maturity, and ability and willingness to be led by their peers. What I did not expect was to see Tequiles take over the rehearsal, and put to use all her experience as a performer who understood the seriousness of the moment and what it demanded. Tequiles Celestin was a very talented actor and dancer who had performed many times on the Hamilton stage and outside of school. She was a very down-to-earth young lady. She was very friendly and had a smile that would light up the room. She was well-known and respected by her peers for her kind disposition and for her extraordinary talent. It is no surprise she would go on to become Miss Tuskegee University three years later. But on this day while I was talking with some of the other student volunteers, Tequiles, hearing the steady noise and sensing the lack of seriousness and concentration, began to yell passionately at the students on stage and those around her that they know we have a show tomorrow, and what we are doing now will not be tolerated and will cause us to have a terrible show, and that's not what any of us want. "WE NEED TO FOCUS ON WHAT WE ARE DOING! STOP ALL THE SIDE TALK AND PLAYING AND GET SERIOUS SO WE CAN PUT ON A GOOD SHOW!" she shouted. She told many of her music academy peers that they know better and this is not how we prepare for a show. Hamilton has a very popular Academy of Performing Arts (AMPA is what it's called now), but back then it was just the Music Academy. About 65% of the BSU students attend Hamilton, then and now, because of AMPA, so when she addressed them, they knew she had credibility because they had performed together and knew the standard they must uphold. She would not let the cast bring less than their best effort because this was not an actual Hamilton Music Academy production, but "only" the BSU show. There were no more issues after that. However, because we started planning the show so late, we were still not sure how things would go when we finished rehearsal for the day. All we could do now is get a good night's sleep and be ready for tomorrow, show time.

Hamilton High School students attended four classes a day for 90 minutes each, and then a shortened last period which was seventh period. The block schedule called for students to skip two of their six classes per day. The show was scripted for seventy minutes, which allowed time for classes to enter and be seated and/or exit and be ready for the next class period. We would perform this show for each class period. The students arrived for the 7:15 call time and there was an air of excitement and anticipation in the auditorium. I felt it as soon as I walked in. The first show was to begin at 8:15 so students were going over lines, dance routines, and tightening up any last-minute details before going backstage. The classes began to arrive as the entrance music played from the sound system over the auditorium speakers. I had attended the previous BSU shows as a teacher bringing my class, but this was different. I was now responsible for the show and I knew the behind-the-scenes work that went into the preparation, and the uncertainty that comes with hoping everything goes right. Once the classes were all seated, I could see that there was standing room only in the auditorium which had a capacity of about 575. Every seat was filled and there were still classes waiting outside hoping that a teacher didn't show up and they would get a chance to be seated. The BSU show was a highly anticipated event on campus. All of the ethnic shows were. I believe that because there were so many BSU students in the Music Academy and the talent was so rich among our students, the Hamilton community couldn't wait to see what was in store. I also believe the students did a good job of promoting the show on campus, especially since this was truly their production. One could imagine their own excitement about that new reality.

The audience was treated to amazing performances by our Hamilton dance students under the leadership of Ms. Latrece Douglas and some of her top dancers including Bria Taylor and Uyoata Udi. Ms. Douglas has led a dance program that I believe is second to none in the city of Los Angeles. Bria and Udi were two of the dancers that I got a chance to meet during the preparation for the show. They are extraordinary talents and one can see the love and passion for their craft when they take the stage. The students are well trained in choreography and hold their peers to a high standard even when Ms. Douglas is not present. Her influence is hard to miss when watching her dancers, and her fingerprint (or footprint) has been on every BSU show that we have performed. In addition to the dance performances, the show featured a monologue by the very talented actor Zeno Robinson who performed his piece from the microphone in the sound booth, (I learned it was called the "God mic"), over the silent showing of blacks suffering during the Jim Crow era. There were powerful spoken word pieces and acting skits all knitted together with seamless transition pieces by the hostess Kambria, who was a natural on stage and kept the audience smiling and glued to every movement of the show. Because of the way our schedule worked, there was one show, then the nutrition break, then two more shows, followed by lunch. The last show for the day was after lunch.

This would be the way our shows were scheduled each year. By the end of the day after the fourth show everyone was tired, but the weariness could not compare with the exuberance that came with knowing they just made history. For the first time the BSU students wrote, directed, and produced their own BSU show and it was a huge success, not to mention they did this all in just a few weeks. I was extremely happy for the students and very proud of them. They deserved all the accolades they received from their peers and the faculty, and they received a lot. One fellow teacher told me that she had been at Hamilton for close to thirty years and this was the best BSU show she had ever seen there. In the years before, the Black History program, as it was called, was organized by teachers and featured performances by poets and our dance program, but it was not done by the Black Student Union. The leaders had watched these shows during their high school years and some did participate, but it was not their production. BSU had not had a presence in the Black History program at Hamilton High School until that day in February 2011, and for the students, this was their moment. For me, this was my first time and this was all I knew. There would be no turning back. If I was going to continue as the

BSU sponsor, and I had every intention to, the Black History program would be a production by the Black Student Union. I have met many BSU sponsors over the years and some have shared that while they do have a Black History program in February, the BSU doesn't run the show. I did not understand that until I realized that was Hamilton too once upon a time. Let me also say here that the Black History programs prior to that year were fantastic shows and done very well by the teachers in charge. As a teacher in attendance, I thoroughly enjoyed them. Now was the time, however, to take the next step and empower the talented students to become co-creators of the show.

The after effects of the show were truly something to behold. In the days and weeks that followed there was a blossoming pride among the students at what they accomplished and a spreading interest in joining the Black Student Union by other students. I realized that the BSU show was the biggest promotional event for BSU. It was the one thing that they did that the whole school could witness. It was a showcase of the talent, the intelligence, the culture of black people. There was a momentum of the BSU on campus that hadn't been experienced before by the members. During the previous years there was a challenge keeping the students engaged. They had sponsors but the extent of their involvement was minimal in relation to what the students wanted and needed. The students wanted to pull together and build the club, but there was no galvanizing force that brought them together and guided them toward being a true student union, a close-knit family that moved throughout the school year with an agenda and goals they wanted to accomplish. That's what they wanted, but they didn't know how to create that. Taking ownership of the BSU show was the first step toward achieving this in that now they had a production they could work toward. They could all participate in it and promote it on campus as something that the BSU does. Students could now associate that wonderful and exciting show with the BSU and that made many want to learn more about BSU. The problem was after the show in February, what was next?

I was still the sponsor, still very new to this role, but I had such a great experience with the students with the show that I wanted to get to know them on a deeper level. I had been used to, and had become very comfortable establishing and building relationships with students. This came very natural to me. I had spent years as a basketball coach and teacher at schools that ranged from middle school to college. Working with young people was my life's calling, so when the void came with the show being over and the uncertainty of what to do next, I felt this is where I can begin to make a huge difference in this club. I decided that we are going to continue our weekly lunchtime meetings in my classroom, and that I would facilitate, and fully participate, in the discussions on a wide range of topics of interest to the students. It was not going to be "meet in my room and please keep it clean I'll see you later." These meetings would be our time to bond and connect with each other over lunch, laughter, and great conversation. Someone might start off with a question like, "How do you guys feel about interracial dating?" The students would take it from there chiming in with their opinions, debating, giving their own personal examples, following up with additional questions, and the next thing you know the bell rings. Other times the students would come in with a burning topic they just had to share with the group. Sometimes it was about whatever was going on in society or in the media with the popular celebrities. The meetings were so fun that when the bell rang to end lunch the students didn't want to leave. Those who wanted to know more about BSU and possibly join were invited to come to the meetings and some did.

I really enjoyed these meetings and getting to know the students of the BSU, and also letting them get to know me. I would share some of my experiences as well because I wanted them to know that I too am human, from the same neighborhoods as many of them, with some very similar experiences. Therefore, I could relate to them, yet also give them perspective from someone who's been where they are with guidance (that's what they wanted), that could help them on their journey. We couldn't wait until the next week to meet again, but also you could see how they got along outside of the meetings because we were building relationships and you could see the impact on the students. I also took notice that the younger students were coming and getting more involved in the conversations.

One of the early topics of discussion was more of a serious note. That school year the Los Angeles Unified School District, facing a budget crisis, began handing out Reduction in Force (RIFs) notices to teachers throughout the district. Hamilton was set to lose many teachers and the Music Academy would be greatly affected. The students talked about rumors of who we might be losing and how they felt about some of their teachers. These were also good conversations as I would hear some of their stories about my

17

colleagues and how they felt about their classes. This decision brought out the best in our student body. The faculty was notified that the students were planning a school wide walk out in protest of the decision to lay off some of their favorite teachers. I personally was not aware of this until the day before. They had used social media to plan and organize this walk out and it was a concentrated group effort led by our very own ASB and BSU President Portia. On March 11, students peacefully walked out of their classes and began their march around the perimeter of the school. Literally all 2500 plus of them participated in this peaceful, inspiring, and well-organized walkout. They had water stations spaced out throughout the route. They shouted out their call and response chants. They had their signs prepared, and they had even coordinated with the local news stations to be present at the gathering spot on the steps of our Norm Pattiz Concert Hall, our auditorium. Now this was not a BSU event, but it speaks to the kind of student leaders in BSU, as I know Portia and Tequiles were among the organizers. On the steps of the auditorium when everyone had finished their trek around the school perimeter the student leaders gave speeches in what was called the "Save Hami" demonstration. I stood in amazement and pride as I watched the students passionately and peacefully fight for the jobs of their teachers. They showed me how much they care about our school and the entire Hamilton community. They also showed their ability to organize and use their voice to bring positive change and fight for what they believe in. I was honored to be associated with such an inspiring group of students. The grand finale of the event was when Jazmine Williams took the stage in white face paint with black lipstick and black tears painted running down her cheeks. Jazmine was tall with a light complexion and had a gracefulness about her. She looked like she could have been dancer, but she was a different kind of performer. She was a very talented spoken word artist and had performed in the BSU show as well as over the school P.A. system for Dr. Martin Luther King Day two months prior. That is when I first heard her and I knew I had to meet her. Her poem to Dr. King was enough to bring tears to your eyes. She had a way of performing where she would recite from her written speech and then toss each page or note card to the floor when she was finished with it. This is what she did that day during her impassioned and emotional speech. I stood there thinking that one of my best career moves was getting involved with these amazing students. The whole student body had witnessed a great BSU show and now they were witnessing this monumental moment where some of the same BSU students were organizers and played major roles. Then they would see some of those same students in weekly meetings when they were just down-to-earth students having a good time with one another. The BSU momentum was growing in the spring of 2011 and the light grew especially bright within two young tenth grade students who found a place in our meetings. The impact that BSU had on these two students is still being felt today.

As the semester progressed toward June and graduation, I began to think about the leadership of BSU and how the new leaders would be chosen. I really had no idea so I asked the current leaders how the new President was selected. At that time, they told me it was simply passed on from the current President to whoever wanted it next. Basically, whoever wanted to be President would make that known to the outgoing President, and that person would make the decision. That is what they did. They informed me who the next President would be, and I was ok with that. I knew who the heir apparent was and I thought she was worthy of the role. There were two younger students, however, who approached me and told me they wanted to be the co-Vice Presidents. They had been attending the meetings and they were really excited about being a part of BSU. Even though they would only be juniors the following school year I admired their passion and enthusiasm, so I rewarded that by naming them co-VP's. Most of those leadership roles were taken by seniors, it wasn't like there were many leadership positions in BSU. That structure simply did not exist in the club at that point. There was a President, Vice President, Secretary, and Treasurer. That was it. That would change soon.

The new President, which was announced before the school year ended, was Jai Williams. Jai was the younger sister of Keara, who had recruited me to be sponsor of the club. Jai was a very talented dancer in the Music Academy. She had performed in the Black History program as well as many other dance productions. She was an equally hard-working and ambitious student. She had a kind disposition and every time I saw her, she was in a good mood, or at least appeared to be. Always ready with a smile, she was very easy to talk to, and like the previous leader she had the respect of her peers. I would not say she had a very close relationship with her newly appointed Vice Presidents, but they had a great deal of respect for her. I doubt that Jai could have anticipated what would happen with BSU when her reign began in the fall.

The two soon-to-be juniors were Alexander Wilson, Jr. and Selasie DeSouza. These two young men were good friends who took a strong sense of pride when it came to BSU. They were both children of immigrants. Alexander was of Afro-Caribbean descent. His mother was from Ethiopia and his father from the island of Curacao. Selasie's parents were both from Ghana. They were both very good students. They were really involved in the school community. They played on the sports teams and had lots of friends on campus. Alexander and Selasie became frequent visitors to my classroom during breaks. I got to know them both really well and they seemed to appreciate the role I played in their school experience. In me they found a black man on campus in whom they trusted and could look to for guidance and mentoring on a variety of issues. I didn't have the same relationship with Jai which was fine because she didn't need that from me. Jai had very specific goals she was trying to achieve as her junior year was coming to an end. She was focused on her college application process and being the best dancer she could be. Periodic check-ins were all we needed, and I made it clear to her that I was there if she needed me. The heavy lifting would be done by her two strong and determined Vice Presidents. This was the leadership of BSU that we were ready to take into the next school year. I think it's safe to say the BSU had found their sponsor and I was looking forward to the new year.

This experience as BSU sponsor for that semester taught me the importance of empowering the students. I learned early on that there are times I have to step back and trust what the students bring to the table. This was clear to me during the preparation for the show. I had no experience of any kind with productions like that, so I had to trust them. They had performed many times on that stage so I had to learn from them, and I had to be ok with that. At the same time though, because I was ultimately responsible, I needed their respect which I was able to earn by developing those initial relationships. They respected how I empowered them, but still guided them, and they in turn showed me they can be trusted to put a show together, and it worked. I learned the importance of making sure in our meetings that students felt safe enough to express themselves and that all opinions would be valued. I had to be explicit and intentional in how I protected each student in the meeting so that no one would be attacked. I had to be the central figure in that process. I had to be someone the students could all look to for leadership, which meant I had to be all in with this club. It was not simply using my room and the occasional check in. If I am going to do this I must be fully committed. I also learned that as the seniors fall back in the spring semester, the younger students must be encouraged to get more involved and even take leadership roles. They must know that they are as much a part of BSU as the seniors. This creates a sense of excitement as the new leaders emerge and gives everyone a feeling that they are part of something bigger than themselves. This first semester for me could be considered the birth of the modern BSU at Hamilton High School. We were just beginning a wild ride.

2

Resources and Relationships

I come from a large family. My dad, Johnny Turner, was born in Georgia and spent most of his childhood going back and forth to Florida to stay with extended family. He had six siblings. He was the third oldest of the seven Turner children. He left the Southeast as soon as he was able to join the United States Navy and that is what brought him to California where he met my mother, Patricia Anderson. My mother had eight brothers and sisters. She was the second oldest of the nine Anderson children, and by all accounts she was more like the second mother to the rest. I have lots of cousins on both sides of my family. Though I haven't been to Florida and Georgia in many years I do keep in touch with that side of my family. The Andersons are all living in the greater Los Angeles area so I see them a lot more. My maternal grandmother, the late Ella Majors was the matriarch of the Anderson family after marrying one the earliest black firefighters in Los Angeles, my late grandfather Charles Anderson. It is this larger Majors family, (my grandmother and her siblings), that kept us all together during my upbringing, and after many family gatherings and reunions, it was now time for the grandchildren to become the organizers of those family activities. I assumed the role of the family historian and our next family reunion was scheduled for the summer of 2011.

I spent the entire 2010-2011 school year researching the Majors family history. The highlight of all this was to have my daughter by my side on many occasions explaining to her the lineage into which she was born. Being able to show her pictures and tell her stories of her ancestors was a memory that I will cherish forever. The reunion took place in the summer of 2011. Throughout the entire process of researching the family history all the way to the actual reunion I began to take notice and develop a deep appreciation for the women in my family. By the time we began the 2011 fall semester that appreciation had grown into a strong focus and desire to learn more about black women throughout our history. This desire merged with the lingering question of how could we duplicate the success of last year's BSU show, and then it hit me. I thought to myself, "What if we did a BSU show paying tribute to black women?" There was certainly the content with which to educate our audience and I knew we had the talent to make it entertaining. Why not? This would be different than any other show I've seen, and certainly any other Black History program. But it should be. We could not tell the black experience in one seventy-minute show nor would we try. I decided at that point that we would give the audience a different aspect of black history and black culture each year. This year would be our tribute to black women. I had a strong feeling that when I approached Jai, Alexander, and Selasie about this idea they would be on board. Time would tell.

One of the first activities of any club at Hamilton is Club Rush. Approximately a month or so into the school year this event takes place on the quad and it is quite a spectacle. Each club is given a table or booth by the Associated Student Body to set up during lunch. ASB has the layout and assigns each club to its particular spot. Hamilton has a grass quad in the middle of campus and on each side of the quad there is a walkway bordered with sitting areas along its path. The south side of the quad has benches along the grass side and large potted plants and trees that border the other side of the walkway. Outdoor tables and chairs are interspersed between the foliage and these serve as popular hangout spots during nutrition and lunch. The east end of the quad is bordered by benches that go along the edge of the grass and this is the widest of the walkways and is bordered on the other side by the pergola, where outdoor seating is situated under a large canopy. Though the pergola is on the other end of the quad opposite the stage, one can have lunch there and still have a good view of what's happening on stage. The north side of the quad also has benches situated along the edge of the grass and on the other side of the walkway, and lastly there is the west side of the quad with its lower flat concrete performance area in front of the steps that lead to the elevated stage. There is no back wall to our stage, so behind it you can see some of our most ardent basketball enthusiasts who play every day on the courts that lead to our small gymnasium. The stage and quad are open areas where most of the school population can see and/or participate in any big event on campus. Club Rush is such an event. There are on average about 50 or more clubs on campus each year, and BSU is just one of them. On Club Rush day, the school is buzzing with excitement. The custodial staff and ASB students can be seen during the period before lunch bringing out the tables and chairs for all the clubs. Club leaders and/or representatives are able to get out of class a little early (in most cases), so they can set up their respective tables usually with posters, balloons, and anything else that can bring attention to their area. Some representatives bring food to entice fellow students to come to their table, but it is all about promoting your club. We have thirty minutes to get as many students to sign up for our club as we can, and when that bell rings, it really is a rush.

The tables were situated all around the quad bordering each walkway and the area in front of the stage. Some tables were even behind the stage. BSU had a location that was not along either side of the quad. The BSU table was located on the south side of the quad, but along the open driveway that separated the quad from the covered eating area. Because there were so many clubs this area was used as well, as it was one of the main routes from the front to the back of the campus. The BSU table was situated at the front end of this long artery, and ironically it was where traditionally all the football players hung out. It was known as the "senior tree." On any given day during nutrition or lunch this was a heavily populated area. On Club Rush day, particularly this fall, it was a mad house. The entire quad area was filled with students roaming up and down each walkway stopping to sign up and hear about the various clubs, and to grab a bite of whatever they were offering. Along the side of the covered eating area there were also gatherings around each table, and then there was the BSU table. There were posters and signs everywhere and there was Alexander and Selasie leading the gathering, helping form the lines, and getting more people to sign up for BSU that day than ever before.

By the end of lunch, it was clear to me that things would not be the same as last year. During my first semester with BSU we had about 20-25 students who made up the entire club. When I finally got back to my classroom with the sign-up sheets, after our area had been cleaned up outside, I sat there momentarily to let my excitement calm down. What had just happened was really incredible. It was an amazing thing to see that level of excitement about BSU. We didn't have food to entice students to our table, we didn't have music to get anyone's attention. All we had were students who, because of their outgoing and vibrant personalities, were able to attract their peers. That detail cannot be overlooked. I started counting the sign-up sheets and when I finished we had a total of 165 students that had signed up for BSU during that thirty-minute lunch period. There was representation from every grade level, particularly with the ninth graders. I knew right then that our entire structure had to change.

First of all, I knew that there was no place where we could meet weekly that could hold over 165 students. We couldn't hold our meeting in the gyms, nor could we use the auditorium. That was the second item on my priority list. The first was to order BSU t-shirts. I had seen someone wearing a BSU shirt from a previous year, but I had only seen that on one student. Whatever they did have before, there was very little remnants of that on campus now. I enlisted the help of Jearena Calix, a former player of mine when I coached basketball at nearby Dorsey High School. Jearena and I developed a very close relationship while I coached her, and by the time the playing days ended we were more like father and daughter. It is still that way to this day. Jearena owns her own business designing and printing shirts and other marketing products for schools. She was the perfect person to approach about the BSU shirt idea. I had seen a design online that I really liked and I wondered if she could do it. Not only was she able to duplicate the design, but she experimented with the font and colors to make it unique to our school. The design featured a fist punching through the front of the shirt as if it's coming at the viewer. The fist is surrounded by the words "Hamilton High BSU." She made me a few of these to wear at school and the students loved them. She made some in different colors, red, black, green, and gold. She also made me a blue one. I got the idea to have different color shirts to represent the different grade levels, and this helped me somewhat solve my other problem, the meeting space.

My classroom was the normal meeting place before the explosion in membership. The room was located in what we call the "Lab building." The main building, known as "Brown Hall," faces Robertson Boulevard, a main street that travels north and south from the Santa Monica Freeway through West Los Angeles into West Hollywood. Hamilton is located at the southern end of Robertson on the west side of the street with Brown

Hall facing east. The lab building sits right behind and parallel to Brown Hall. Between the two buildings there are outdoor tables and benches where many students congregate during the breaks. The west side of the lab building opens up to the center of the campus and by far the most crowded area during lunch. By extension the lab building was a main hang out spot as well. This particular year the administration decided to close off the lab building during lunch because there had been too many reports of bad behavior in the building. The plan was to only allow students in the building if they were in a club or some meeting, and had to be verified by a teacher. Our adjustment to this new policy was to create BSU passes that would allow the students in the building at lunch so they could attend the meeting. In addition to this I had to go to other teachers in the building who might allow a small group of our BSU students to meet in their room. The plan was to break up the group and have different grade levels meet among themselves in different rooms. Three teachers volunteered their rooms to help us out and that is how we conducted our meetings. Initially I would give them a topic to discuss so all of them could talk about the same thing, but later I realized I should just let them have their own discussions. I would go from room to room and check in to see how things were going. For the foreseeable future, this is how we would meet. There were separate rooms and different color shirts for each grade level.

It was now time to meet with Jai, Alexander, and Selasie to tell them what I was thinking as a theme for the BSU show. By the end of the semester, I had done lots of research on black women in history and I knew the audience would appreciate such a tribute, and learn a lot. As expected, the BSU leaders thought this would be a great idea for a show and began to think about how we would organize the show. We enlisted the assistance of two of our BSU students who showed a lot of leadership among the group, and who were both amazing dancers in their own right. They knew what it takes to put together a good show and they were great at working with their peers. They knew who to recruit and cast to make sure we had the best students for each act. Jonathan Anderson and Deshaunna Dorsey were two amazing dancers. They were committed to their craft. Both not only performed at Hamilton, but were also in outside productions. They were also scholars. They knew everyone we needed to give our audience the most entertaining show possible. Jonathan did most of the writing and producing of the show while Deshaunna helped recruit the talent and direct. Deshaunna did not play. When students did a good job rehearsing a dance, a song, or a line from a skit, she would let them know. But when they didn't, she would also let them know. You wanted to make sure you had been practicing when it was time for Deshaunna to watch your performance. She had a way of telling you to get back to work and didn't care who was listening. Interestingly enough, in my role as sponsor I was waiting for someone to come to me complaining about how Deshaunna talked to them, or how she made them feel, but no one ever did. I saw the look on the faces, but they would go right back to work and make sure they were better the next time. Whether it was the respect factor or the credibility Deshaunna had among her peers, she proved she was the right person to bring the most out of her peers in that stressful space of preparing for a show like ours. Jonathan and I worked together a lot on how the show would be formatted having lots of discussions on show order to make it most effective. He was committed to the vision and deserves a lot of credit for writing the show that year. The great thing about working with these students was that egos were never a problem. Jai, Alexander, and Selasie never had an issue with

Jonathan and Deshaunna taking the lead during the month of January and February when we were in full show mode. Much of our lunch meetings focused on details of the show which is always scheduled at the end of February. Jai was cast into the show and was totally fine with following directions even though she was President. President Harry Truman once said, "It is amazing what you can accomplish if you do not care who gets the credit." That quote captures the attitude of the student leaders of BSU that year. It was truly a team effort and no one seemed to care who got credit. They were determined to put together a good show because they saw what last year's group did and now it was their turn. And since they didn't care who got the credit then, I am giving them all credit now.

The annual all-day rehearsal on the day before the show was now a day filled with excitement. One reason for this is that after weeks of rehearsing lines, dance routines, and skits on their own, it was now the first time to see it all together in a live run-through. Another reason is that they get to have the full day out of class and enjoy a day in the auditorium with their peers. Work aside, it truly is a fun day. A highlight of that day for me was hearing the voice of Bethany Watts for the first time. Bethany was a friendly tenth grader who always greeted me with a smile. She had a pretty smile and every time I saw her, she seemed to be simply enjoying high school with her friends, Jasmine and Monica. The three of them were always together. On this day, they were in the auditorium on stage, as it was their turn in the show order that we were trying to go through. I was in the sound booth in the back of the auditorium as the sound and light technicians were getting their cues in preparation for tomorrow's show. I learned a great deal from these students who were assigned the job by their teacher to work our event. As the sound tech cued the music to "Pieces of Me" by Ledisi, this tenth grader with the pretty smile goes into "People just don't know what I'm about," the first line of the song. My jaw dropped. Evidently everyone knew Bethany could sing because as they cast the show they all heard her. I wasn't there during casting so I didn't know. I had never heard that song before that moment, and when I found out what it was I later played it. One could not sound more like Ledisi on that song. I was blown away by this talented young lady. I got so excited because all I could think about was the reaction of the audience tomorrow when they hear Bethany sing that song.

We had some strong performances in store for our audience, beginning with the singing of "Lift Ev'ry Voice And Sing," which is how we begin every show. That song always sets the stage and gets the audience in the mood for what they will see over the next hour. Our goal was to go back to the days of slavery and highlight important black women in American history all the way up to the present. We had strong spoken word pieces by Christine Dawson who recited "Ain't I A Woman," by Sojourner Truth and an original piece by Tiffany Davis called "She's Cute, For A Dark-Skinned Girl." Our amazing dance team treated the audience to their exciting routine to "Wade In The Water." I can still see the dancers in their white costumes as they wove seamlessly on and off the stage jumping, kicking, and splitting through their movements with the grace and energy that kept the audience on the edge of their seats. That was all before Bethany sang her song. With Jasmine and Monica as her background singers, Bethany sang that song with passion and power and received a standing ovation from her peers. What a talented group of students! There were short monologues read by students who played the roles of great women like Mary McLeod Bethune and Elizabeth Eckford of the Little Rock Nine. There was even a section of the show where students paid tribute to great black mothers. By the end of the show, we made sure to shout out the black female teachers and faculty on campus. It was a beautiful gesture and well-deserved. It was another great show! We had given the audience an educational and very entertaining show, and by many accounts we had even outdone the previous year. Another show was now behind us and just as the one last year the student's felt a great deal of pride, and many more students who had not been in BSU were now coming to join.

The BSU Show took place at the end of February but we had the entire Black History Month prior to the show to promote and learn about Black history and culture, as well as enjoy one another. A new thing we began that year was to attend the annual Pan African Film Festival. This was a great event during the month that had previously been held in Culver City, and was walking distance from Hamilton. My students and I had walked to the Pacific Theater the year before as a class field trip. The Pan African Film Festival brings dozens of yet-to-be-released black movies to Los Angeles to be screened. It takes place over about a two-week period, and a portion of the show is dedicated to showing movies to students in a program called Student Fest, where students get to view one of the movies for free if they come as a field trip. Although various teachers took their class as a field trip, the Black Student Union never went as a group, until now. This would become the second event that we could call our own BSU event, and because it was another annual event, we now had two things we know we could plan to do every year, the BSU Show and attend the Pan African Film Festival. This particular year the festival moved from the Pacific Theater in Culver City to the Magic Johnson Theater at the Baldwin Hills Crenshaw Mall. This was perfect for us because the students could go to the mall and have lunch after the movie. The Student Fest called for the showing of the movie at 10am. The movies were rarely longer than two hours so we had time to have lunch at the mall and get back to school by 2:00 which is when we were required to have returned to school, and since Hamilton was only about 15-20 minutes away from the mall, we could hang out until about 1:30. In the mall there was the food court of course, but there were also different booths set up throughout the mall where you can buy African clothing, jewelry, and art. The advisors are given a choice of movies to view as part of the Student Fest program and this year I chose to see *On The Shoulders Of Giants*, a documentary about the first black basketball team, the Harlem Rens, and written by Kareem Abdul- Jabbar, who was at the showing of the movie and stayed after to answer questions by the students in attendance. This was a real treat for us, as Kareem is such a knowledgeable man on many subjects, and who couldn't benefit from hearing him speak about his documentary, basketball, and the Harlem Renaissance era? With the Pan African Film Festival taking place in mid-February, it gave us an opportunity to get away from school and enjoy a day of fun, which by this time was much needed due to the stress of planning the show. The bonding that takes place on such a trip cannot be overstated. At the festival, we are typically allowed a certain number of seats in the theater usually because other schools will be present and they wanted there to be enough space for everyone. It was my goal to take approximately 50 students, as that's how many could fit comfortably on a school bus. I had to ask the Student Fest organizers for permission to bring that many students, but they were very accommodating. The problem I would face, since our group was so large now, was how to decide who to take to this field trip. It was important to me to include students of every grade level on this trip, but at the same time I knew this would be a memorable experience for our seniors. I decided that I would reward those students who were regular attendees at our lunch meetings. This would become the deciding factor on most field trips going forward. Though we did not schedule many trips at that time, those who attended the meetings would be the first to receive invitations. However, even with that policy, there may still be additional room, and then how would I decide? With approximately 200 students, there wasn't room for everyone to attend meetings even with the four rooms. I wanted to make sure students who couldn't always make a meeting knew that they were still a part of BSU. I explained to them that their biggest contribution to our BSU, the most important way to validate their membership in BSU is carry themselves with respect and character on campus at all times. They may not always be able to make a meeting, but they can always do that. And that became the expectation for all members, to represent our club with class and integrity. I had to take an active role of getting to know each member so that if there were issues with teachers or other students, they could come and talk to me, and I would help guide and build that character. Providing guidance was more than giving direction to the club, but also helping each individual member, and this was a critical aspect of building relationships with the students. Therefore, I would sometimes select students for field trips who best represented the club through their actions on campus, or even feedback or comments that I would get from faculty about a student. At that time, these were our only field trips, but later there would be more, and I would have to continue to look for ways to make sure as many students who signed up for BSU would have opportunities to go on trips and participate in other activities.

It was expected that BSU would have its strongest presence of the year during the month of February since it was Black History Month. In the fall semester, by the time Thanksgiving arrived the focus was clearly on preparing for the show in February. From March until the end of the school year there was not a lot that we had planned other than to continue meeting and strengthen our club with that quality time. I thought about going back to meeting as a group in one room, but I had to find a room much bigger than mine. My room was small and only had about 15 desks which was all I needed for my classes. Since we could not find a space that semester, we kept meeting in separate rooms. By the end of the school year, I realized that what made last year such a success, the togetherness, was being threatened by my decision to separate everyone in order to accommodate the size of the group. I realized that we could not continue to meet like this, and the summer break came at just the right time to re-evaluate and form a new plan when we come back to school in September. Besides, it would last for only about two months because after spring break and then later the senior prom, the seniors did not attend the meetings as much. I noticed the decrease in senior attendance, but the overall attendance stayed the same, as younger students were attending more. This happened naturally. I noticed it, but it wasn't until later that I would factor that into how we conducted our club business. This was yet another thing that I was learning about how to run a club. The only thing left to do at that point was to focus on the transfer of leadership going into the next year. Since we had two co-Vice Presidents who would both be seniors the following year, it made sense that one of them would assume the position as President. I didn't have to make the choice at all as they approached me with the plan that Alexander would be

President and Selasie would be Vice President. That was about the same time that Jai informed me that she had been accepted to, and would be attending UCLA in the fall. I remember having the same conversation with Portia the year before. She had a goal of attending George Washington University, and eventually becoming the American ambassador to Ghana. Unfortunately, she did not get in to GW, but she did get in to Boston University. Here now was my second President on her way to UCLA where she would again be joining her sister Keara, my favorite Bruin. I was extremely happy for both of them, because they were very close and I knew how happy they were knowing they would both be at UCLA together. Now with Alexander and Selasie returning to lead BSU, and with Jonathan and Deshaunna returning also, next year was shaping out to be one to really look forward to. By now they were all going on their third year in BSU, and we had established the kind of club we wanted to be, and they were all in.

BSU this year was about resources and relationships. In my second year, my first full year, I learned a lot more about the resources I had on campus. Those people who were in positions and had certain talents and skill sets that could help me lead this dynamic group of young people. First, I had the respect of our Principal Gary Garcia. Mr. Garcia had been watching our club operate, and had seen the response to the BSU shows. He and our Assistant Principal Betty Washington knew we had a positive message and they saw the impact on the black students on campus. They became a source of support for me and things I wanted to do with BSU. Similarly, Ms. Zuccarro who was our Music Academy Director, was instrumental in organizing the school wide assembly. She orchestrated the teacher sign-ups and organized the seating chart in the auditorium. She offered her assistance and support throughout the preparation of the shows. I appreciated her support and valued her knowledge and expertise, and we built a good working relationship. Ms. Chorna was the Music Academy teacher who assigned the students to work the sound and lights and stage management crew. These students were critical to our putting together a good show and were well-trained and very good at what they did. We too had a good working relationship. I cannot overstate the respect and admiration I had, and still have for Ms. Douglas, our dance teacher. The BSU shows would simply not be the same without her. The dancers that perform in our shows bring an element of drama and excitement that make it a truly unique experience for our audience. I treasure that relationship I have with Ms. Douglas. It's also important to learn the resources right there within the club. The students have talents and skills that they can use on stage, but many of them also have skills in such things like public speaking and organizing, and even cooking. These skills can be used in many ways as you will see throughout this book. I've learned that people are my most valuable resource and building relationships with those people must become one of my strongest abilities, not just for what I can gain from them, but also for what I can bring to them.

3

Building a Team

"I need you to be strong for me." That is what she said to break the eerie silence as I sat there with my body and mind trying to decide whether to be shocked or go numb. That silence followed my mother's sharing with me the news that she had been diagnosed with pancreatic cancer. I knew cancer to be a deadly disease, but also one that people can survive. I was not aware of all the different types, and I had no knowledge of pancreatic cancer. I began to research the literature only to realize just how serious and deadly this form of cancer is. "But not Patricia Turner, she would be one of those who survived this," I convinced myself. It was September of 2012 and that was my mindset as the school year began.

There was an air of excitement around BSU on campus coming into this school year. Those two enthusiastic sophomores from two years ago were now leading the BSU. President Barack Obama was campaigning for re-election. This group had spent their entire high school career having a black President of the United States. That had a profound effect on the young black men that I worked with at Hamilton. His presence, his power, and his position showed that being educated, articulate, and informed on a variety of subjects can lead to unimaginable success. There was something else that I took particular delight in, even though my mother was constantly on my mind, and that was the fact that my daughter Kenya was now in ninth grade and attending Hamilton.

I was already so proud of her for so many reasons, and now I got a chance to see her at school every day and go on this high school journey with her. She had always gone to relatively small schools, so Hamilton was definitely something she would have to get used to. Hamilton had an enrollment of approximately three thousand students at that time. On the first day of school Kenya was in my classroom in the morning when it was time to go to her first period class which was P.E. She was very nervous, as was the case with many new students, especially from small schools. I decided to walk her to the gym where the classes were meeting, and when we entered the gym, there were more students sitting in the bleachers than she had ever seen in any of her previous schools. The adjustment would take time, but I knew I was going to enjoy every minute of it. I had also just taken a job as an assistant women's basketball coach at nearby West Los Angeles College. This was shaping out to be a very interesting and very busy year, and it was just beginning.

Our BSU enrollment had surpassed two hundred students last year, but we lost a lot of those students when our class of 2012 seniors graduated. We wouldn't know just what the numbers would be like this year until Club Rush later in the month. What I did anticipate was that the number of students would be at least the same as last year, but I expected even more. With those kind of numbers I had to think about the structure of the club going forward. With Club Rush nearing it was brought to my attention for the first time that all clubs needed to have a written constitution on file with ASB and in the student store with the financial manager if they were planning to do any fundraising, and since ASB wanted all clubs to fundraise, the constitution was not optional. The mandate for the constitution was very much in line with what was clearly our BSU moving from a club to more of an organization. This was one of those details that I missed early on because I should have known this last year. Nonetheless, the constitution called for naming the officers and up to that point we really only had a President and Vice President. We had students who were tasked with putting together the BSU Show but they were not considered officers during the previous years. Now we had to specify who held what positions, and not only did we have to, but it was necessary for such a large group. There needed to be several students with specific leadership roles and those roles should be made clear to the rest of the group. I began to think about how to organize the structure of our BSU and I drew from my experience as a member of Alpha Phi Alpha Fraternity, Inc. With a goal of developing leaders, as is part of our mission, I decided that we would build this organization around three guiding principles: scholarship, leadership, and service. First of all, I wanted to make it clear to the students that their participation in, and ownership of, their education was why they were in school, and that nothing comes before that. I wanted to challenge them with that truth so that doing their best in that area was the expectation and not a suggestion. In turn, I would do everything I could to help them in their academic endeavors, such as writing letters of recommendation for colleges, exposing them to college opportunities, and making college going culture a big part of their BSU experience. That meant that we must schedule events that would help them in their college pursuits, and that is exactly what we did.

Secondly, I wanted the students to see themselves as leaders and embrace opportunities to step up and take leadership roles. Even if they did not have leadership roles, I wanted them to participate and speak up when they had opinions, validating that they too have something meaningful to contribute to whatever group they find themselves in. If for no other reason that leadership was one of our principles, it was so that the BSU students would think like leaders when it comes to making important decisions, and not follow the wishes of others. I wanted them to at least be leaders of themselves. Lastly, I wanted the students to have an appreciation for what it means to help those who are less fortunate, or even less knowledgeable. I wanted them to embrace opportunities to help those in need, and to have that as something our BSU is known for was very important to me. This now became another thing I must schedule into our year because we can't say that service is important and not show it in our actions. In the previous years there were only two BSU events and that was during February, but with our new guiding principles we now were able to start looking for activities throughout the year that would help us live up to those principles, but first we had to assign key leadership roles to students who were ready and willing to lead this organization.

With the positions of President and Vice President intact, I had to find a Secretary and a Treasurer. Also, with the anticipation of hundreds of members, I felt we needed to add committees to the organization, so we could meet in smaller groups for specific purposes. The new committees would be the Black History Program committee, the Fundraising Committee, the Community Service Committee, the Social Activities Committee, and the Constitution Committee.

Additionally, I felt it was necessary to make sure that students of all grade levels had representation on what we would hereafter call our BSU Executive Board. There would be two students representing each grade level from ninth through eleventh. There was no need for twelfth grade representatives because the officers and many committee chairs would likely be seniors. This body would be structured with senior leaders in many positions.

For Secretary, I decided to appoint a fun-loving and down-to-earth cheerleader/dancer named Destany. She had approached me about being Secretary, which was starting to happen more and more as BSU was growing. Students would come and inquire about having a certain role of leadership. This was another policy that had to be written into the constitution so that the process would be very clear going forward. Destany had a lot of school spirit and she was very committed to BSU. I knew Destany would be at every meeting. She was organized and would be able to take good notes of the things we talked about such as plans for BSU events. She would prove herself to be very valuable later on. For the position of Treasurer, I chose a student who was again becoming very fond of the BSU and that sense of empowerment that comes from being a part of something special. I could see this happening and it was exciting to witness. This student's name was Mia. She too was a dancer and cheerleader and a good friend of Destany's. The Treasurer would be the student who kept track of the money we had in the BSU account in the student store. If we raised money, or wanted to spend some of the money that we did raise, the Treasurer would have to take the money to the student store for deposit, and sign off on any money that was to be spent by BSU. This is obviously a position of enormous trust, but Mia took this role very seriously and proved herself to be trustworthy, which should be a primary characteristic of the student given this position. I also created another board position called Financial Secretary. This is the person who would actually be the point person to collect and handle the money at any school fundraiser such as Back-to-School Night or Homecoming. Another student committed to BSU and was always present at our functions was Dominique, and she was my choice for this position. I believed that it was of major importance to have another set of eyes on the money, which would create more transparency. The main people who would keep track of BSU funds were the President, Treasurer, Financial Secretary,

Fundraising chair, and myself. With transparency as our primary objective, there has never been an issue involving BSU funds.

The role of the committee chairs would be to hold meetings with smaller groups of BSU students with the focus on the business of that particular committee. It was a chance for students other than the President to lead meetings, and also plan specific events that BSU would hold both on and off campus. The Black History Program Committee would have the purpose of creating, writing, producing, and directing the BSU Show. This was an enormous task and required students who understood that this production is our most spectacular event of the year. It is the one thing we do on campus that is seen by the entire school, and therefore it is where we showcase what BSU is all about. The chairs of this committee were those who put the show together, but the committee itself was really made up of those students who wanted to be a part of the show. It was our objective to produce a show that would have as many students as possible participate. Because our Music Academy was so popular, and with approximately 65% of our BSU being members of the Music Academy, lots of students came to audition for roles in the show, many for on stage roles, but also several for behind-the-scenes jobs. The show brought everyone out. The chairs of this committee had already been decided, and with Jonathan and Deshaunna returning I knew we would have a great show. I added a third person, Jelani, to help because I saw how talented she was as a member of Amazing Grace Conservatory, a performing arts consortium where Kenya participated during the summer months the past several years. Jelani was also a leader who understood how to put a show together, and had the respect of her peers. As of the beginning of the school year, however, we did not know what the theme of the show would be. Those ideas would be fleshed out through the months of September and October, as we wanted to know exactly what our plan would be before Thanksgiving. As for the Fundraising Committee, I thought it was important to have some way of raising money for the club, even though I was not sure how we would use the money. Up to this point, nothing that BSU did required the use of money, but I was sure that once we had money, we would find ways to spend it. The Fundraising Chair would have to lead that committee and gather fundraising ideas from the members and present those to the Executive Board so they could make decisions to move forward with the plan.

Then the Fundraising Committee would execute whichever ideas were chosen. The Fundraising Chair position was given to a very enthusiastic eleventh grader named Maya. This was a very dedicated student who, when learning about the different positions of the board wanted to take on multiple roles. She felt as though she could lead in several positions. We settled on two positions for Maya. She would chair both the Fundraising and the Social Activities Committees. The Social Activities Committee is the committee that plans all the fun activities for BSU. They would organize our Black History Month activities, except for the show. If BSU were to host any event that brought the whole club together, the Social Activities Committee was responsible for doing the planning. Some events might also be fundraisers in which case they would work with the Fundraising Committee in the planning. If an event were also a community service event, they would work with that committee. One of the great benefits of this new structure was that it allowed the committees to work together and that philosophy has remained with us to this very day. The Constitution Committee was designed to meet for the purpose of drafting the constitution as well as making sure we operated based on this agreed upon constitution. Every Executive Board member was required to read and sign the constitution before it was to become official. Board members had the right to challenge any item in the constitution and we would then have that discussion in the board meeting. Once all have signed the constitution it becomes our working document for that school year. Each year the committee would look at it and decide if any changes should be made before signing. This committee would have to view this document as something that would last long after they graduate and it would require them to consider in great detail how they wanted to structure this organization. They would have to be students who held the organization in very high regard, to be protected and viewed in the same manner by future students. The chair had to exemplify this characteristic. I chose Erika for this position for all of those reasons. Erika had the maturity, communication skills, and the respect of her peers to hold them and herself accountable for producing this important document. Although I played a lead role in the creation of the document, the students worked with me all the way through until its completion. The last committee appointee was the Community Service Committee Chair position. Like all the others, this committee was very important, especially since one of our aims was the idea of service. This group would brainstorm ways in which our BSU would give back to the Hamilton community. The leader of this committee would have to be someone with a service mentality, one who finds joy in giving back, and who is willing to not only lead, but work. I found that person in a student named Amber. Amber was a genuinely kind person who never had anything bad to say about anyone. She was always willing to help, and she really sought out this position. She was a natural fit.

The grade level representatives consisted of two students of each grades 9-11 who were considered leaders of that class. These were students who would be asked to recruit students from their respective grade levels to join BSU or, if they had already joined, to come to our weekly meetings. They would also help get important BSU information to their grade-level peers as well as provide feedback from those peers to the Executive Board. They would also be asked to lead their grade-level meeting discussions. This gave even more students the opportunity to lead meetings and facilitate discussions. This is one of the main reasons our BSU has been able to maintain large numbers of students each year. Giving younger students an opportunity to lead creates a stronger interest and more of an ownership stake in BSU. I believe this is the best way to develop leaders, by giving them opportunities to lead. The representatives for the junior class were Maurissa and Alexus. Cory and Destiny were chosen as tenth grade reps, and my daughter Kenya and her friend from middle school, Melanie, were chosen as ninth grade reps.

In addition to structuring the Executive Board we also had to have more structure to how and when we would hold our meetings. We decided to have our first meeting of the year on the Wednesday after Club Rush. This is when we would know all the students who had signed up to BSU and this would probably be our largest meeting of the year. I was successful in getting permission to use the auditorium for this meeting. We would continue to have our regular meetings on Wednesdays in separate rooms, but there would be committee meetings held throughout the week. Each committee chair would schedule the best meeting day for them as well as how often the committee would meet. The Executive Board would meet on the last Friday of the month to discuss BSU business. During these meetings, the President would give a report as well as the committee chairs, and the grade level representatives. This meeting is where all BSU decisions were made. Once the constitution was read and signed by all Executive Board members, we were ready for Club Rush and ready to test out this newly structured organization that we called BSU.

Club Rush was actually the second event that the BSU would participate in at the beginning of the school year. The first was Back-to-School Night. This annual event takes place about three weeks into the school year and became for us an opportunity not only to raise money, but to promote the club. During Back-to-School Night certain clubs would set up tables around campus in certain buildings, walkways, and other high traffic areas and sell items such as candy, pizza, coffee, or other refreshments. The key was to find a highly visible area, set up posters, and bring a lot of attention to the table. Students had to be welcoming and friendly and to represent the club in the most positive way, and our students had fun doing that. Parents would stop by, purchase an item or two, have a brief conversation with the students, and walk away feeling that this is something they wanted their students to be a part of. It was a great way to make an impression on the parents as well as others who didn't know much about the BSU. Since we hadn't had Club Rush yet, the table was manned by our Executive Board members, particularly our financial secretary, but any board member who was available could help out. The table was set up not far from my classroom so that when I had no parents in my room I could easily go and see how things were going. Inevitably I would have to stop and have a conversation with an interested parent, which I was always excited to do.

The day had finally arrived and the Club Rush scene was in full effect. This was my second time seeing this event and it seemed even more crowded than last year. By now there was certainly a lot of interest in BSU, but it's not until you see the crowd around the table that you really understand the popularity and excitement that this club has generated on campus. I had to step back and appreciate the way that Alexander and Selasie, and now so many others made BSU a really cool thing to be a part of at school. When the thirty-minute lunch period was over and all the sign-up sheets were brought to my room and counted, we had signed up over 220 more members to our BSU. After seeing the crowd and looking at the names of the students on all these sheets I challenged myself to make sure that every student who signed up for

BSU benefits from that decision one way or another. I had to not just wait for, but seek out, opportunities to keep the students engaged, encouraged, and motivated as long as they were members of this club. There was simply too much interest, and too many students for this to be just another club.

After Club Rush our first meeting was the following Wednesday in the auditorium. The plan for this meeting was to have the members of the Executive Board introduce themselves to the general body and talk about the upcoming BSU events. I began the meeting by welcoming the over 200 students in attendance and sharing with them our principles of scholarship, leadership, and service, and that is what this club is about. I also shared with them that while it is important to attend meetings as much as possible, the best way to represent this BSU is by how you carry yourself on campus, meaning being respectful to yourself and others and being a positive contributor to the campus culture. Once I finished my welcome, the students took it from there. When the meetings are properly planned out the students feel much more comfortable to lead. The planning of the meetings is very important. One of the events that was mentioned by the President was to be our next event, the BSU mixer. This is where all those students who signed up for BSU can come together and sign up for the various committees we had, all while listening to music, eating, and getting to know one another. This event was scheduled for the following week in an empty classroom, and was another good time had by all. It accomplished the task of having new members join committees so they too can become more involved, and it is also a way of seeing emergent leaders among the club. So, over a period of three weeks we had Club Rush, our first meeting, and then the BSU mixer. Now it was time to begin our regular weekly meetings. We continued to meet in separate rooms at this point. Each grade level in their own respective rooms with the smaller committee meetings and Executive Board meetings being held in my room. I was successful in getting permission to use the auditorium for the first meeting of each month, which did allow us to all meet together at least once a month. The Executive Board meetings would be held on the last Friday of the month and they would serve as the planning meeting for the next Wednesday, the first Wednesday of the month. This system worked for the first semester, but it would still not be as good as having one meeting space. We would finally get that later.

One of the great things that happened for our BSU that year was my developing a working relationship with Ms. Monroe. She was the head of our ESL office, and she had become very fond and very supportive of our BSU. She loved the BSU shows and would often present opportunities for our students to either attend an event of some kind or to participate in some performance. She had a dance background herself and was deeply interested in the performing arts. One of the first events that we were able to attend that year was an invitation from Ms. Monroe to walk a few blocks from the school to the Kirk Douglas Theater to see a live stage play about former boxing champion Jack Johnson. This was a great opportunity to enjoy time with the students, and them with each other. There were about 50 students and 5 staff members and we all really enjoyed the performance as well as the bonding time. This would be a precursor to the types of events that Ms. Monroe would present to us, but our working relationship would really grow with the time we spent planning and eventually executing the district's first African American Family Day.

My typical schedule consisted of leaving Hamilton right after work to go to basketball practice at West L.A. College. Kenya, who was now on the volleyball team had practice after school. Once I got out of practice, I then returned to Hamilton to pick her up and then we would go home. Some days I would take her and my son Isaiah to visit my parents who lived really close to us, but these were only the days when my mother felt up to it. I would call and see how things were going on a daily basis, and I was so upbeat and so thankful for every good day. The visits to the doctor and the chemotherapy were taking a toll on my mother, but she was a fighter, and the strength in her voice was so encouraging to me. Little did I know that her condition was getting worse. Kenya had finished her first high school volleyball season and we were just starting our basketball season around Thanksgiving of that year. It was a small family gathering at my parents' house and it happened to be Isaiah's birthday. There was the usual family laughter and great conversations that we had all been so accustomed to when my mother told my dad she had to go to the hospital. My dad, my brother Wayne, and I all went to the hospital to be with my mother. They decided to keep her, and that following week I was going to the hospital every day. I would drop Kenya off at school and then go visit my mother at nearby Kaiser hospital.

Then one night while preparing for a game at Cypress College I got a call from my brother. "Ken, mom's not going to make it." I yelled back into the phone, "What do you mean?!, What are you saying to me right now?!" I didn't know how to process what he was saying. I could not focus on anything after that phone call. I coached the game, and immediately after, I went into the locker room and broke down in front of the team. There was never a time in my life that I can remember crying like that. I have never felt so helpless. For the first time, it had resonated with me that I was losing my mother. That Monday, I decided that I would take Kenya to see her grandmother in the hospital and I am glad I did. My mother passed away at 2:00am early Wednesday morning on December 5, 2012. I did not share this with Kenya that day because she was in the midst of taking her final exams early. I took her to school that morning, and while I was there, I got a chance to see a student of mine who was in the office with his mother. He was not a BSU student, but he was in my class. This student seemed to always find it necessary to have his mother at the school. If he wasn't getting into trouble in class, it was because of some negative behavior on campus. Before leaving school, I could not pass up the opportunity to speak to him about my current situation. I sat down with the student and his mom and said, "Let me share something with you. My mother died this morning. But you know what? Before she finally left this earth, she got to see her son become a successful adult, have a family and a good career. I want you to look your mother in the eye and promise her that she will see you do the same." His mother sat with tears in her eyes as he made that promise. Time will tell if he keeps his word.

I took the rest of the semester off and would not see the students until January when we returned from Christmas vacation. When we did return, I received a great deal of support from everyone at school, my colleagues, my students, and especially the BSU students. There was a certain amount of stress because like my first year, here we were in mid-January with a BSU show to plan for February and nothing in place as far as a plan or a theme. And just like two years prior an unlikely event happened. A student, this time a current student, happened to catch me in my class after school. It was Destany, our BSU Secretary who wanted to talk about her concerns for the show. Destany had performed as a dancer the previous year in the show, which was outstanding, and she wanted to make sure we had another good show. Jonathan and Deshaunna were involved in another project that kept them from committing as much time to our show and so there was a void there. However, as is customary with our BSU, another student, in this case Destany, stepped up. This was not her role at all, nor did I suspect that she was that interested in the production side of the show, but here she was. We sat there and discussed some ideas and since I always think about ideas for a possible show theme, I mentioned to her, "What about making President Obama the theme of the show?" She liked the idea, and we began to brainstorm a timeline of significant events that would have been impactful in President Obama's life. We included key events in the Civil Rights Era, the Black Power movement, college scenes, even Motown. We also included excerpts from some of his speeches, and before you know it, we had written "From Reconstruction to Re-election," our newest BSU show and I was really excited about it. Destany took it from there. She was instrumental in selecting the cast, organizing the dancers, and helping direct the show. When we communicated the plan to Jonathan and Deshaunna, they were grateful that Destany stepped up, and gave whatever assistance they could to developing the show. It was a huge success. In this show, we featured a step-show during our college scene. We had a Motown scene that again feature Bethany from the previous year. This time she and her background singers performed "Come See About Me" by the Supremes. We featured our Hamilton Choir who performed "Battle Hymn of the Republic" at our Inauguration scene, and we even had our own BSU President Alexander portraying President Obama. To that date it was our most popular show. We received lots of praise school wide on how well the show was produced with all the features included, and also the timeliness that just a month prior to the show, President Obama had given his second inauguration address. We definitely captured that moment in our show. In addition to executing our show, once again we had a chance during that month of February to do some of our other activities. We attended our second Pan African Film Festival field trip, this time seeing a film called *The Last Fall* about a football player who was looking for one last chance to make it to the professional level. Another new activity we were starting this year was Greek Week. One of my goals was to get the members of the Divine Nine Black Greek Letter Organizations to be involved with our students by coming to speak and share the many great attributes of their respective organizations. Even as a teacher it was important to me to bridge the gap between the community and the classroom. I've always thought as an educator to make everything in school relevant to what the students might experience after high school. Since I am a member of one of those organizations and I know members of the others, I thought that would be a great way to start connecting our students to people from the community who could inspire them. Greek Week would feature different organizations visiting each day of the week during lunchtime. Not only were these members able to speak about their organizations, they also spoke about the careers they held, and about college culture, all things that motivated our students to pursue college with renewed enthusiasm. Greek Week was then, and has continued to be a great addition to our annual activities. We even added a Spirit Week in there which included wearing certain clothing on certain days. For example, there was African Attire Day, HBCU day, and there was Black Friday in which the entire BSU work black on that day, included in that was the wearing of our BSU shirts every Wednesday. Now our February calendar was filled with activities that lasted throughout the month, giving our BSU great visibility and exposure, and I emphasize that it was good exposure. Everything we did on campus during the month was positive, inclusive, well-publicized, and it all led up to the BSU show at the end of the month.

Entering into March many of the students who put a lot of time and energy into the show got a chance to rest a bit. All we had planned was our regularly scheduled Wednesday meetings. I did find a vacant room upstairs that had enough space for about 50-60 chairs plus a long counter in the back for more seating. When I found out the room was vacant it became an easy solution to our problem, about as good as I could hope for. We moved the meetings to room 612 and as many who could make the meetings would show up. Sometimes chairs were put in the hallway so students could still hear. This is that time leading toward Spring Break when the seniors begin to focus more on their end of year activities, particularly prom. There were two more changes that this year's BSU would see that would be new implementations for years to come. One of our alumni, much like Keara years before, was now working at Hamilton in our UCLA office. She was a current UCLA student named Ameinah. She approached me about a program they were doing with selected high schools called "Buddy Day." This was a field trip where high school students would visit UCLA's campus and meet with students from some of their Black Student programs. The high school students would then partner up with their UCLA "buddy" and shadow them for the day. That meant they would attend class as well as any scheduled or non-scheduled activity with their buddy. Sometimes it meant just taking a tour or visiting the dorms. After a few hours the group would reconvene, have lunch, and then a panel discussion before heading back to school. This was a trip we scheduled for after Spring Break. This was an opportunity to take students who were not seniors on their own field trip, thus giving me a chance to bond with the underclassmen more and help create that buy-in within that population. I took students of all grades on this trip and it proved to do exactly what it was intended to do, motivate the students. On the bus ride back to our school I remember Chrystal, a sophomore talking about how the trip impacted her, and what she needed to do to position herself to get accepted into college. She was extremely impressed and I could hear the excitement in her voice. She had been motivated and inspired more than any person talking to her could accomplish.

Immediately I knew this would be another annual event of ours. It was the beginning of what would be a strong relationship between UCLA and our BSU.

The other new implementation we added this spring was our new election process. Our first three presidents, Portia, Jai, and now Alexander each had done an amazing job, but since our BSU membership had grown to consistently about 300 students, and more students wanted leadership roles, it was now time to have an actual election process to select the next President. I had decided to appoint all the positions on the Executive Board except President and Vice President. The Vice President would be selected among those who did not win the President position. Each candidate for President would have to submit an application that I created. They would have to write an essay explaining why they should be selected as President. They had to submit a letter of recommendation from a faculty member, and then they would have to be interviewed by the rest of the Executive Board who had already been appointed by me. This to me insured that this position would not be based on a popularity contest, but actually earned by someone who is committed to fulfilling the role. There were two students who emerged as candidates for President for the following school year. One was already serving as 11th grade rep. Maurissa was a very sweet person with a beautiful smile and an incredible singing voice. She too had graced the stage during the BSU show during a protest scene in which she sang "We Shall Overcome" as students walked down the aisles of the auditorium with lit candles, and as the auditorium screen showed footage of Civil Rights marches. It was a powerful and moving scene, and now that same Maurissa was running for BSU President. The other candidate was not an officer but had been very active in BSU beginning with her presence way back in October during Homecoming. Camille was one of the students who carried the banner for BSU during the Homecoming parade, which at our school was a daytime event since we didn't have lights on our field for evening games. Not only did Camille carry the banner but she was a loud and strong voice as she walked around that field. Her voice and her advocacy for BSU was just as strong after the parade for the rest of the school year. Camille was a spoken word artist much like Maurissa was a singer. She was artistic and creative and lent those talents to the BSU show as well giving the audience one of her spoken word pieces. She was vocal in meetings and she had the respect and admiration of everyone in BSU. Both of these candidates were very smart, kind, and mature. Either would make a great BSU President. They had both submitted everything that was required and it was now time conduct the interviews. Each student on the Executive Board would ask one of the pre-written questions then they would all score each answer based on the scoring system on the list of questions. They could score each answer as high as a four, meaning they loved the answer, all the way down to a zero, for a non-answer. There was also a place to comment on the answer. There was a total of 15 questions, and after all the interview sheets are added the candidates end up with a total. The next step after the group interview is a personal interview with me in which I go in knowing who the board has chosen based on their interview sheets. My meeting is usually to confirm who the board has chosen, or make the final decision if the candidates were evenly scored. In this case, the board spoke and it was clear that Camille was their choice for President, even though they loved Maurissa as well. After Maurissa enthusiastically accepted my offer to be the Vice President, we now had our board with the exception of the 9th Grade Representatives, who would be arriving next fall.

The last thing we did for this exciting year of many changes was to congratulate our departing seniors with Alexander and Selasie heading to UC Riverside and UC Merced respectively. Jonathan was on his way to San Francisco State University and Deshaunna was off to Tuskegee University. Those four students were extremely instrumental in these first three years of establishing a BSU and having it grow from a few students to a few hundred. They took a club and helped form it into an organization. Now this organization was poised to have an even greater impact on its members and the school at large.

Year three was a year of many changes within my personal life, and the BSU. It was a very emotional year, and I can't say that I learned this during that year because I already knew it, but those students were there for me when I needed the strength to continue after the passing of my mother. They gave me great hope, not just in their future, but in mine as well. My mother was always proud of the impact she saw that I had on the young people I taught and coached. I pledged to her that I would continue to always make her proud. I grew close with many of the students that year. Having Kenya there with me meant everything. I got a chance to watch her grow that year. She had a very good volleyball season. I met many freshmen that year and those seeds of leadership were planted. I saw many leaders in that group. Many of them hung out in my classroom every day during the breaks. We developed a special bond and Kenya was right there witnessing it all. It was as though our bond was strengthened as we both grieved the loss of my mother.

When asked to create a mission statement, our President wrote something from his heart that best described the essence of what BSU had become just three years after we began. For anyone looking to start or grow a BSU, the key is in the first sentence written by Alexander. "BSU is not just another union. Through our informative discussions we seek to enlighten our members; through our weekly meetings we seek to teach self-discipline and responsibility, and through our annual Black History Month program, we seek to empower and advocate the improvement of every race, but especially African Americans." The first thing to realize is not to see your BSU through the lens of what's already present at the school site. We must see it for what it could be. We have to reimagine what school clubs look like and can look like. Alexander was right. This wasn't just another club. Our BSU was now in a position to have an impact beyond our campus. We were ready for the challenge.

4
Consistency and Stability

Three years ago, when Portia stood on the steps of the Norman Pattiz Concert Hall and passionately called upon each class to represent that they were indeed present and in support of the Save Hami demonstration, I stood there as she yelled out "CLASS OF 2011 MAKE SOME NOISE!" By the time she got to 2014, I remember how surprised I was to hear how loud and enthusiastic the freshman class was. It was a few weeks after our BSU show and there was the President urging them on. This was their first year of high school and it was turning into a very exciting year. Those freshmen then had now become seniors. It was fall of 2013 and this senior class had spent all four years witnessing the growth of the Black Student Union. Over the past three years they had seen the shows, attended the meetings, had attended field trips, and heard from guest speakers, all in the name of BSU. This was the class that I started with. Neither they nor I knew much about a Black Student Union when they entered high school. This year we were able to see how much we've grown together.

The year got off to a somber beginning as the news circulated around campus that one of our very popular football players, who had just graduated that spring, had been shot and killed in a drive-by shooting days before the beginning of school. He happened to be good friends with our newly elected BSU President Camille, who in true fashion went immediately into the school year with a plan that would honor the fallen star, his legacy, and give BSU a theme for years to come. She decided to use her artistic talent and design a T-shirt that would promote a message of peace and non-violence. We would sell these shirts and the proceeds would be donated to the star's family. On the front of the shirt were the words, "Guns Down Voices Up." This message was meant to encourage the community to solve problems and disputes peacefully and not resorting to fighting, which often leads to gun violence. It was also a call to action for everyone to speak out against the gun violence in our community. The back of the shirts showed open wings with the characters "B24" in the middle, which stood for the star's first initial, (his name was Bijan), and his uniform number. It also meant to be at peace 24 hours a day. At the bottom of the wings there was written "Hamilton BSU Los Angeles, CA." This act set the stage for how our BSU would be led throughout this year. There was a deeper commitment to love, peace, and togetherness and it was emanating from our President. There was a positive perspective that Camille could find in every situation. She was not one to let setbacks and discouragements bring her down. She had an uncanny way of staying focused on the positive, and the whole club fed off of it, including myself, and I'm always positive. I know that is why the two of us worked so well together throughout the year. Working with Camille was like working with another colleague instead of a student. She was that mature, and her peers saw her in that same light. She was to that point the most involved of any President in all aspects of the BSU. She had a hands-on approach that allowed me to see for the first time, a President truly take ownership of the club. This is not to take anything from any previous Presidents. In fact, I think part of her disposition was learned from watching those Presidents. She saw that this, at some point in time, would be her club and she was going to make sure she had her fingerprints all over it. We begin with our first activity, Back to School Night.

We had set up our table in our usual high traffic area right in the middle of the Lab Building, just steps away from my classroom. This was probably the center of all the traffic when the parents came to our campus. It was also where the ASB usually set up their table, so I knew it was a good location. We have a Financial Secretary who has the responsibility of being the money collector at any event where we are raising money. Therefore, the President doesn't necessarily have to be there, but this was Camille. She stayed at the table with the Financial Secretary and served as the perfect ambassador for the entire two-hour event. As people passed by or came to our table to purchase one of our evening snacks, Camille answered questions and urged the parents to get their students involved in BSU. She had such an inviting personality, and a charismatic way of communicating that everyone who visited our table walked away extremely impressed and excited about getting their students involved in our BSU. When I was able to, I stood there with her and we enjoyed every minute of promoting our club, and the bonding that was taking place between us and the other members of BSU who joined to help out and just be a part of the evening. I began to develop a long-term vision about where this BSU could go and the ultimate impact it could have on the members and on our campus. I knew that we were being led by one of the most respected, admired, and well-liked students on campus, and her impact would be felt for years, this I could see.

One new addition we added to the beginning of this year was a slight change to our usual Club Rush plan. I had developed a very good relationship with a woman named Nicole Ford, who owns a company called Stepping In The Right Direction. This company takes students from California on HBCU college tours where they get to see the campuses and meet leaders of black colleges. This gives our students quite an experience. This year Nicole and I agreed that when we have our table set up for Club Rush, she would have a table next to ours promoting her tours. Students would sign up with her to show interest in attending a tour, and then Nicole's staff would follow up with the student and their parents to arrange for the student to attend. This turned out to be another huge success. We had our, now usual, turnout of hundreds of students signing up for BSU, but there were dozens who also signed up to go to Nicole's tour and many more who didn't sign up, but had lots of questions and learned a lot from her. Nicole is an HBCU alumnus and is very passionate about giving California students the opportunity to see and hopefully attend black colleges. In fact, one of the students who signed up to attend the tour, which was an October tour that happened to be during the time of Homecoming festivities for most of the colleges, had a lifelong dream of attending UCLA. When this student went on the tour during October, a little over a month after Club Rush, she came back and said to me, "Mr. Turner, I want to go to Tuskegee." She was so amazed and felt so inspired during her visit that it completely changed her course, really the course of her life, and she decided to attend the prestigious HBCU. That student was Maurissa, our Vice President. This alone was worth bringing Nicole to our school to promote her tours, and many more of our students have since attended HBCU's because of this relationship. This is an important benefit of BSU's establishing lasting relationships with people and businesses in the community.

After Club Rush we had our usual first meeting in the auditorium where the leaders were all introduced and there we announced our mixer which would take place the following week. Just like we did the year before, the plan was to bring everyone together and give them an opportunity to meet the committee chairs and join the various committees we have. This time the mixer would be in the small gym. The committee chairs all had tables set up around the gym and we had music, food, and we even brought a TV over so we could show footage from the previous year's BSU show for those who might be interested in being a part of this year's show. Lots of students signed up for the committees we have and now it was time for those committees to begin the work. One of the committees I want to highlight here was the Community Service Committee led by Nala McAdoo. This committee planned and executed a very successful Thanksgiving Food Drive and Giveaway that year. The plan was to donate food, but not just canned food and non-perishable items. They decided to actually cook food and prepare meals and give those meals away. Many parents contributed either ingredients or cooked meals, or both. I even cooked a huge pot of spaghetti. We planned the giveaway for the day before

Thanksgiving. We had tents set up on the northern end of the front of our campus where there was a grass area in front of our auditorium. We had several tables where we kept the food warm in trays and we had containers ready to serve the food. A business owner across the street made special signs, which was his business, and gave us those signs to promote. There was a home nearby where older veterans were cared for. They saw what we were doing and came over and got some free food and talked with our students. There were those who pushed carts down the street collecting recycled items to redeem for money. They came and got some free food as well. There were people driving by in cars who stopped to give well wishes and donate money, even though the food was free. We even fed our dance team who had been practicing in the auditorium getting ready for the Winter Dance Show in a couple of weeks. They came out after their rehearsal and got some free food. When it was all over, we had given away over 100 containers of meals. The students felt an amazing sense of accomplishment and gratitude that they were able to help so many people, and we had a lot of fun doing it. This kind of community work also serves as an excellent opportunity to bond. This is exactly why I wanted to include service as part of our guiding principles. That day the students clearly experienced the joy in serving others.

Earlier I mentioned the importance of building relationships with people and businesses in the community. I need to include in that statement the importance of building those relationships with the local colleges and universities. The previous spring, we had gone to our first UCLA Buddy Day. That relationship from that time had been firmly established and we had scheduled to attend our second such trip with an opportunity now to have a fall and a spring Buddy Day. Since we were now going to be able to do this twice, I decided that the fall trip would be just for seniors because this was the time when they were actually applying for college. I decided to make the spring trip specifically for 10th graders. That meant students who attended Buddy Day as 9th graders last spring would get to go again this spring, since they were 10th graders. So most of our seniors, including Camille and Maurissa, got to go to UCLA during this fall semester and it was a good experience for the seniors because it emphasized our goal to make scholarship a priority. Not all the seniors who attended had chosen UCLA as one of their top colleges, but sitting in those classrooms, nonetheless, gave them a clearer sense of where they wanted to apply and what to look for in a college. Being on a college campus gives students a better understanding and a clearer vision of how they view themselves as college students.

Another relationship that led to a great opportunity for our BSU that year was formed with one of our teachers. Ms. Connie Moore-Kelly, an African American math teacher at our school was a huge supporter of our BSU. She had a brother who was a famous musician, and either through that relationship or one that she created on her own, we were introduced to a jazz drummer named Laval Belle. Mr. Belle and I met at the request of Ms. Moore and he said that he wanted to do a free concert for our BSU. We could charge for the concert, but he wanted no money from us. This would allow us to promote BSU on and off campus and I was very excited that he wanted to do this, for no other reason but to give us another great BSU event to promote. Not only was Laval going to perform, but he was also bringing with him as a special guest performer, famous violinist Karen Briggs. What I thought was a kind gesture from someone who wanted to support our BSU turned into us promoting a concert from some major stars in the music industry. This was not an event that we came into the year scheduling. We did not know this opportunity would present itself. But it did show me that when you are building something great that has the reputation for doing amazing things for students, people take note and want be a part of it. They will lend their expertise to help those who are doing great things for young people. I was coming to realize that very clearly at that time. Our BSU was simply working to maximize every opportunity for the black students at Hamilton, and people were taking notice. It was very exciting to see. On the night of the concert, Laval Belle and Karen Briggs put on an amazing show for the spectators. The fact that we have a renowned Music Academy was not lost either. Our amazing jazz band puts on concerts all the time so people are used to seeing performances in our auditorium, but this was different. This was a BSU event and the professional musicians were incredible. It was an event that proved to be the perfect way to finish off a busy semester. We had been active since the beginning of the school year and by late November we had done enough for an entire school year, but we had more to do. The exciting thing was the event that we had spent almost a year preparing for was coming soon, and it was not the BSU show which we are always excited about. This was African American Family Day coming in January, and our BSU was to play a big role in that event. Christmas vacation came at the right time because we were in for a busy second semester. And we couldn't wait.

While sitting at a training one day with colleagues from Hamilton along with representatives from many schools, I heard one of the presenters mention some activity they hosted called "Black Family Forum." It was described as a Saturday event that brought the black students and their families to discuss certain programs in the school and how best to serve the black students. This was very interesting to me especially since the presenter stated that the school had less than 50 black students enrolled. I immediately thought about what something like that might look like at Hamilton. Ms. Monroe, who was also present at the workshop began working on procuring a grant that was designed to provide funds to be used for our black student population. She was successful in getting the grant and her idea was to create African American Family Day. An event that would be hosted at Hamilton and would bring together our black students and their families for a day of learning about various services and programs offered through Hamilton and our feeder schools.

The Saturday event would only last about four hours, but it would include workshops from some of our teachers as well as outside education professionals. There would be breakfast and lunch served, entertainment, and even day care provided for younger children. It was truly a family event. The first year of African American Family Day had taken place last year during the 2012-13 school year, and almost immediately after that event we began planning for next year's African American Family Day. The event was scheduled for January of 2014 and there were regular meetings throughout the year led by Ms. Monroe. The plan was for this year's event to be much bigger. We were now including not only Hamilton, but several high schools and middles schools in our area. We would still host the event, but there would be contributions from many schools in terms of advertising, finding workshop presenters, providing entertainment, and of course, bringing their families. The event would feature a keynote speaker, and similar to last year's event, an acknowledgement of someone who had been of great service to the youth to receive a special award. The first year we acknowledged Hamilton alum actress Paula Patton. We were all excited when actor/comedian Cedric The Entertainer accepted our invitation to be our special guest at this year's event. We had great presenters lined up for the workshops, and each school had done an outstanding job with outreach to their respective students and families. This year the BSU's at the various high schools were asked to play a major part in planning the student portion of the day. Camille had been present at most of the early meetings and played a key role in giving us the student perspective. With her help we decided that the students would be in the cafeteria while the parents attended the many workshops taking place in various classrooms. There would be a host for the activities in the cafeteria where the students would hear from a panel of alumni from various high schools who were now in college coming back to share their stories of college life and their experiences. There was an open mic session along with live music. On the day of the event our school was immaculate. The custodial staff did a phenomenal job making sure the school was clean and the decorations and all the aesthetics were meticulously planned and designed by the amazing event planner Mitzi. She designed the brochures that would go out to the schools and the programs and notebooks that were used during the day. She decorated the school cafeteria, auditorium and all the places where there would be traffic. She had the food professionally catered. She along with Ms. Monroe and Ms. Dana Henry, who worked with our Communities in Schools Program, deserve all the credit for planning an event with the attention to detail and the care that made all the families feel special and proud to attend. It was a first-class program from start to finish. It was the first time our BSU got to network with other BSU's and learn what other schools' BSU's were doing. I began to see at that very moment that we were doing something that wasn't being done anyplace else. I can still see the shock on people's faces hearing that our BSU membership was consistently in the three hundred's, and at the things we were doing. I had never really thought about what other schools were doing. We were too busy building our brand on campus and creating that space for our students to shine and feel appreciated. I took notice of the many compliments that we received from other students and their families. Our BSU had started to develop a reputation for being a really strong, powerful, and respected group outside of our campus. Without African American Family Day, I doubt that we would have been able to see our impact on other schools.

We had learned shortly before the day of the event that our special guest Cedric The Entertainer would not be able to attend the event. However, he had arranged for the appearance of the co-star of his sitcom *Soul Man,* actor Wesley Jonathan in his absence. The students knew Wesley Jonathan from his very popular film *Roll Bounce* where he played the character Sweetness. Needless to say, they were very excited that he would be coming to our school to speak. What Cedric The Entertainer did do since he was not able to make the event was to arrange for us to bring several of our BSU students to the studio taping of the Soul Man sitcom at a later date. This was a very kind gesture on his part. He did not have to do this. Between African American Family Day in January and the time we went to the studio to see the Soul Man taping in April, we had produced another successful BSU show and enjoyed all of our other Black History Month activities.

We had been preparing all along to host our fourth BSU Show in February, and this one was truly a learning experience for all of us. Our desire had always been to include as many students as we could who wanted to be in the show. We had BSU show directors in place, but this was a year in which the ideas were not really flowing and we could not come up with a clear theme or what story we wanted to tell. We had our team as well as many other students who came with ideas and suggestions, and in the name of being inclusive, too many ideas and suggestions became detrimental to our process. The BSU show team had the idea of doing a "BSU Awards Show" sort of like the Grammy's where there are categories of black excellence and success that they wanted to highlight, and students would play the roles of the nominees and winners, giving us the entertainment that we needed, but when we started to pursue that thought there were more acts that the students felt should be included. As we began to rehearse it was Camille's leadership that began to win the group over, and the show began to take on a different tone. I began to notice two things; that the President, as de facto member of the production team, played a key role in the production of the show, and also that the BSU show for the first time became something that the President saw as part of their legacy. The Show was becoming synonymous with the President unlike in years past. In the first three years the President did very little writing and directing the show. They were given a role and they played that role. This year Camille was much more involved, and in every aspect of the show. She wrote, directed, and performed, and because of her natural inclination toward the idea of being true to yourself, and being truly free to express yourself, that became the theme of the show, which was eventually titled "Married to Freedom." The show promoted the idea of not just individual freedom and freedom of expression, but also the idea of acceptance and allowing others to be themselves, and most importantly loving one another. This was Camille's contribution to the show. It was to be her legacy. What that established in future shows was the precedent that the President could be more involved with the appointed program directors in developing the theme of the show if they wanted to. This was the first time our BSU show, or any other show that I had ever seen, addressed the idea of intersectionality and included the LGBT community for example. The show focused less on black history and more on current issues and challenges faced by students in the modern day. It also addressed what was becoming more and more popular in the news which was unarmed black people being killed by police. The show resonated with a lot of our student body on that basis of so many feeling as though they cannot freely be who they are without judgment or harassment. In that sense, it was another huge success. I thought the show went in a different direction than the past shows in that it was more of a risk to pull this off, but it turned out to be well received by the students overall. We had done it again. I want to add here that the finale of the show was more true-to-form with the other shows and brought it all to an exciting end with a choreographed dance to a Michael Jackson medley. For a show that took more of a serious tone this dance left the crowd filled with excitement. Students who were there still talk about the "MJ" dance from that year's show.

We also got a chance to go to the Pan African Film Festival once again as we continued to make that an annual event. That event for us always precedes a three-day weekend and we take that opportunity to bond with one another, so the students who get to attend always have a great time. It was our third consecutive year going as a BSU and this year we got a chance to invite some of the faculty members who were always such great supporters of our BSU, and they loved the experience. When given the opportunity to include supporters with things like field trips or even ordering extra merchandise like t-shirts, it is so important to remember those supporters. In addition to our trip to the Pan African Film Festival we also hosted our annual Greek Week and spirit week festivities.

When the day came for us to attend the studio taping of Soul Man, we got to tour the set, meet Cedric the Entertainer and the cast, and take pictures. We sat in the studio audience during the taping, and we were having a great time until something unexpected happened. The comedian who kept everyone laughing between takes began to call on people to take the mic and show off their talent, singing, poetry, whatever they did as an art. All of our students of course knew how talented Camille was as a spoken word artist and they began to look for her to take the mic. The problem was she didn't want to, and we all quickly understood that. Camille was not interested in Hollywood in terms of being on stage performing in that setting. She was very deep and thoughtful and much more of a serious spoken word artist. She spoke about issues that really affected people and had no interest in entertaining that crowd that night. However, when the comedian saw that she was someone who had the respect of the audience he urged her to come and take the mic. When she refused, he continued to call her out, and even began to embarrass her by questioning her talent and her desire to "make it in this business." He didn't understand that she had no desire to "make it" in that business. She was on another trajectory, but he wouldn't hear any of it, and the more he spoke the more upset I got. He wouldn't leave her alone, and then she finally got up and went outside. I was furious, but didn't want to make a bigger scene and destroy the evening for everyone, ruin the taping and everything else. I went out after her and tried to console her, and she told me that she would be ok. When I went back in the comedian approached me trying to justify why he was so hard on her. He explained that "you have to want it to make it in this business." I told him that "she was trying to tell you that she wasn't interested in the business. You crossed the line and you hurt a very special young lady." You might imagine that I wanted to say a lot more. What happened after that was just as surprising. After the cast took their last break and before the last scene for the night, we were asked to come down from the audience and be extras in the last scene. Camille and her mother, as well as another parent and myself were seated in the club scene where we were part of the audience at a stand-up comedy event. I don't know if they did this because of what happened, but I do know that throughout the evening Cedric and the entire cast were great. Our BSU was and still is grateful for the opportunity to spend time with them that evening. I am especially grateful my daughter got to be there and meet the cast members. These are events that don't happen often and they make a student's high school experience quite memorable. The event of that night did not take Camille off course in the slightest way. As you will see she went on to have an amazing finish to her senior year.

The last thing we did that year before beginning our work on the next year was attend our second Buddy Day trip to UCLA. We had taken the seniors during the fall semester, and this time I took the sophomores. This would be their special trip. I knew that it was Camille's dream to attend UCLA so I allowed the seniors who had applied to UCLA and had gotten accepted to attend this trip with the sophomores. It would be a chance for them to experience this trip not as applicants any more, but as newly admitted freshmen. Camille was extremely excited to receive the news of her acceptance. There was a moment when she was concerned that her admission was in jeopardy so when she told me the news, I was extremely happy for her. This would be my second President in four years to be attending UCLA. Hamilton has a pretty special relationship with UCLA. Many of our faculty members are UCLA alums. We are one of the schools that are included in much of their outreach to the high schools and therefore many of our students attend the various programs they offer during the school year and during the summer, resulting in a fondness and an excitement about the possibility of attending UCLA. It is usually the top choice of many students at Hamilton across the board, and that is often true in our BSU, except what is also true is how difficult it is to be admitted to UCLA. It might be the most applied to university in the country according to some statistics and so it is very competitive. Unfortunately, there was also an issue regarding the extremely low percentage of black students who get admitted and attend. That is why I applaud their efforts to reach out to high schools and particularly black students. The fact that Keara, Ameinah, Jai, and now Camille have been admitted gives a lot of our students the hope that they too can get it. That is why when one of our students gets into UCLA it seems more of big deal, but it's really a Hamilton-UCLA connection, a "Yankee-Bruin" connection to quote another Hamilton and UCLA alum, and friend of our BSU Mandla Kayise, Founder and President of New World Education, Inc. With Maurissa headed to Tuskegee University and so many of our other Executive Board members and seniors committing to schools, I decided it was time to start letting the entire BSU know how many of their peers were going off to college. I began posting acceptance letters of all the students in my classroom. When we had our meetings in my room and when students would just come and hang out, they would see a wall behind my desk covered with acceptance letters. This had an enormous effect on the younger students. They would gravitate toward the wall and you could hear the comments about who is going where. Then you would hear, "That's going to be me," or "I want to go there." In building a college going culture it is extremely important that the students going off to college are celebrated publicly, not only just to celebrate, but also to show the younger students that college is a tangible, realistic goal to pursue because every year they see their peers going. The second part of that is to invite, welcome, and celebrate the alumni as they come back to visit; have them speak to the current students as often as you can. Whether the students attend a university, community college, or trade school the celebration is always about the student and not the school. It is important to get that message across to the students.

The 2013-14 year was a busy year for our BSU. We started from the very beginning and went through the year involved in the planning or execution of an event seemingly every day. I realized by the end that if we are not careful it can have a real burn-out effect on the BSU leaders. Camille was involved hands-on in everything we did and I could see that it took a toll on her. I learned that it was important to protect the leaders from all the stress of running a club such as ours, which by now had become more of an organization. I learned to allow, and in some cases, make them step back and give some of the responsibilities to other students. If the seniors and leaders feel the need to scale down by the end of the year, they have deserved that and it becomes part of celebrating them. It is equivalent to a basketball player who has had a great game and the coach takes him or her out at the end before the game is over so the crowd can show appreciation. It is my way of showing them how much I appreciate them. For Camille, Maurissa, and our other leaders like Maya and Nala, and all the rest it was a great year. It was the culmination of four years of participation in BSU. It was about consistency and stability. Halfway through their freshmen year they learned that a BSU had a new sponsor. They saw the BSU show. They saw that the club was becoming an actual operating club on campus. They got involved. Not once during their four years did the club become inactive or change sponsors. They only saw it grow more and more each year in membership, in activity, and in stature. Consistency and stability are essential to growing a club like BSU. When we decide to take on a role as important as this it has to be all in. To create that sense of belonging that is so important, the students have to know that being a part of BSU is being a part of something big, bigger than themselves. When a student enters freshman year and joins BSU, will it still be there when they finish senior year? Will the advisor still be there? Will the enthusiasm still be there? Will they experience that growth each year? That year, I became close with a freshman student who had an older brother in BSU in the 2012 school year when she was just in the sixth grade. This freshman shared with me that back then she said she wanted to be our BSU President one day. She was now completing her freshman year, and there is no doubt that she was impressed with and influenced by the personality and leadership that Camille displayed all year. We would have to wait and see if this freshman would become President.

The freshmen of that 2012 year were now juniors and about to become seniors. That first year of high school they saw our Tribute to Black Women BSU show. One particular freshman participated in that show and every show thereafter. She was a leader in that amazing class, and had now submitted her application to be BSU President. She was one of five students who sought the position, but when the process was complete Stephanie Uche Omuson had been selected to be our fifth BSU President. This class had been very involved in BSU since the beginning. They spoke up in meetings, they were great students, they were talented, creative, and I knew the next year would be very interesting. I knew that when they were freshman. They came in ready to lead, and now it was their turn. The new Vice President was Chantel Wiggins. She was an extremely talented student whose sister, Chanel, another extraordinary talent, was graduating with this current outgoing class. Chantel was one of the choreographers of the very popular Michael Jackson medley dance routine that closed the BSU show that year. She was now one of the leaders after being one of the program directors this year. With Stephanie and Chantel as leaders, and with all that talent, the 2014-15 school year was shaping to be another great year of BSU.

5
Strength in Unity

At Hamilton High School we have three main, what we call, "culture clubs." There are other culture clubs but the three most consistent and most stable culture clubs are BSU, LaSO (Latino Student Organization), and the Desi/ASA (Asian Student Association). Each of the three clubs is given a time during the school year to host an assembly, or do a show in the auditorium for the whole school in what is called our "ethnic pride assemblies." Our BSU takes a lot of pride in this show. It is the most anticipated activity of each school year for us. The school year takes the shape of a plot map in literature where there is rising action throughout the fall semester with the climax being the show in February, then you have the falling action, the events leading to the end of the year. This had always been the pattern for us, but at no other time was this crescendo effect more visible than it was this year.

Beginning with the President, this entire class consisted of students who were very comfortable out front. They were comfortable on stage and they were comfortable leading, speaking out. This year provided us with the cause to do all of those things. The constant and almost regularly occurring news of unarmed black men and women being killed by police began to find its way into schools across the country and Hamilton was no different. These events became the topic of conversation in more than a few BSU weekly meetings. It even got to a point when some students told me they didn't like coming to the meetings because they were so negative and depressing. It is important to note here that even though the Executive Board meets to decide on the topic for each meeting, any BSU member is free to make suggestions on the topic either before, or during the meeting. I told the students that they always have the ability to bring a topic, or change the topic at a meeting, but I don't know how many times this has happened. These meetings had a huge impact on Uche and I could see early on in the year the emphasis she placed on having organized meetings. We even tried meeting with the whole group in the auditorium on a weekly basis, as by now the club was approaching 400 in membership. The meetings would start with certain questions and then the club, who had been separated to different parts of the auditorium would discuss and then report to the whole group. I would go from group to group listening in on the conversations, but there would always be an issue with time. Lunchtime is only 30 minutes long and by the time everyone made it to the auditorium we had about 20 minutes to meet. Much like before, meeting in separate groups, especially in the auditorium, was not an intimate enough environment to keep that sense of closeness. Therefore, after several meetings in the auditorium trying to make it work, we ended up back in the classroom, and that would be the end of us meeting in separate groups.

The BSU class of 2015 was a close-knit group. You could see that even if there were no BSU before, this would have been the class to start one. In fact, some of the leaders did start a new club called "Shades of Brown." In this club, led by Uche and Chloe, our Social Activities Committee Chair, the emphasis was to bring girls together to discuss issues affecting them and support and affirm each other. I was asked to be the faculty sponsor of this club and I gladly accepted because it was well organized and it was an arm of our BSU. Virtually every member of Shades of Brown was in BSU, so it would have been easy just to speak about these issues in our meeting. This signaled to me a testament to their respect for BSU in terms of keeping those meetings about issues that all black people were dealing with while separating their meetings which dealt with empowering girls and young women. It also showed the closeness of the group and their respect and affection for one another. This group was much smaller, so they were easily able to meet in my classroom, and being there watching them run their own club (I had no involvement), was admirable.

From the beginning of the year the BSU leaders were doing double duty running two popular clubs, and that included myself, as I was in the fourth year of a special assignment of my own. As a special education teacher, I had been approached about, and I did accept, having a suspension prevention focused classroom where I was given all the students in our department who had behavioral issues and were more prone to being suspended due to various behavioral challenges in their other classes. I accepted the role of taking all of these students in my class and I would be their primary teacher for all academic subjects. So, in my class during any given period you would see all the special education students who had exhibit behavioral challenges. I was approached for this role because I hardly ever sent students outside of my class for disciplinary reasons. I tended to handle those issues in-house through different proactive measures and de-escalation strategies, mainly lots of communicating and connecting with the classes that I taught. I also had two Para-educators, Mr. Meniefield and Mr. Johnson who were with me the whole day, and the three of us made an excellent team, one fit for just that type of program. There may be any number of challenges you will face on the job that could potentially interfere with your ability and/or willingness to keep the BSU going. These are times when I draw strength and resolve from the students. I saw the passion of this group. I saw them as freshmen and I had anticipated their senior year for some time now. They had such pride in the BSU and they showed it in many ways. There was an incident when a girl in BSU had been continuously provoked to get into a fight with another girl, and it finally reached a point where the BSU student was about to engage in this altercation with the other student, that is until another student mentioned BSU, and that she knows better not to fight. In this heightened emotional state, she began to cry and came and found me. She explained to me that she really wanted to fight the other girl, but then she thought about how it would make BSU look. She was clearly angry and very emotional, but thought enough about BSU that it kept her from engaging in a conflict that she later admitted wasn't worth it. Incidents like that always remind me of what this all means to the students. It truly is for many of them more than just a club. It is literally changing the lives of young people, and so when we decide to take on, or give up, the role of advisor, this decision must be weighed thoroughly and carefully planned. We should not start what we cannot fully commit to, nor should we stop without a plan of succession.

In addition to our regularly scheduled events for the first semester, Back to School Night, Club Rush, Homecoming, BSU once again held its own Thanksgiving Food Giveaway, however this year's BSU has the distinction of hosting a few events this year that no other group has organized before or since. The first of which was relatively simple but no other class has taken it on and that was a very successful Halloween Dance. This may be due to the popularity and overall dedication of Chloe, who was quite busy all year. This was a dance held during lunch in the small gym. There was also a costume contest. We charged one dollar to get in the dance, and it was actually very fun for the students. Hamilton is a school that rarely hosted dances during lunch. We had lots of pep rallies but no dances, so the idea was a little different from what the school was used to, but BSU would be the group to make it happen. This was yet another event in the rising action of the year leading to the BSU Show in February. None of the events though would be more of a precursor to the climax than what would take place right before Christmas vacation.

I was approached by Uche and Georgia, another key figure in our BSU and a strong leader, about their desire to stage a walk-out in protest of all the unarmed black men being killed by police across the country. The plan was to hold the walk-out on December 12, which was the Friday before finals week. Everyone was to wear black. There would be signs and posters made. The students would all collectively walk out of their classes at about 10:45. They would exit the front doors of the main building and proceed right along the front of campus to the parking lot entrance. They would then turn left and go the corner of Robertson and Kincardine on the southeast corner of campus. Then they would walk along Robertson heading north and then when they reach the front walkway they turn left again and congregate on the front steps of the school. This was different from the Save Hami walkout from a few years earlier. This event was totally organized by BSU students; it did not end in front of the auditorium, but the gathering took place in front of the front doors of the main building. There were student speakers and even a parent spoke to the urgency of the moment. The entire school did not participate unlike the other march, but the black students (and many non-black students), about 1,500 presented a great show of solidarity. All the students were dressed in black, and with her powerful voice, I can still hear the passion in Uche's address to the student body to continue to fight for justice with the constant refrain of "THIS AIN'T OVER!" reminding the students that this walkout is just the beginning. She was right. She knew all along that in just two short months she would be on the auditorium stage with the whole school in attendance for what would be a different type of BSU Show.

They began working on this show earlier than the past years teams did. The show directors were two very talented performers in their own right. Destiny was one of our very best dancers and had been an outstanding dancer and choreographer in numerous dance shows during her four years. She would be responsible for that part of the show while her partner, another dancer, but a very talented actor and singer as well, Princeton, would help with the script and the acting and singing parts. Uche was also involved in the writing and had the overall concept of the show. This same Uche had important roles in each of the BSU Shows prior to her senior year including last year when she captured the audience's attention opening the show breaking out of chains symbolizing her freedom. This year Chantel would be producing the show and for all the talent that she possesses in front of the camera, this is where she really shines. It was also special to have Kenya in the booth with Chantel and I. We sat in the back of the auditorium with headsets watching the show and communicating with the backstage workers to make sure everything ran smoothly. This is where

I sat every year during these shows and Kenya sat there with me each year learning how the show was produced. As far as the show itself, this would be a continuation of the walkout in many ways. The intent was to bring to the stage an illustration of the injustices the students see and feel as they observe the events in society. The police killings, in the students' minds, highlighted other micro-aggressions and racism they feel and they wanted to tell their story. My role as advisor is to allow them to tell their story, but tell it accurately, with respect to the audience who is there to enjoy the show, and to educate and entertain, always representing what our BSU stands for and means on campus. The students have always respected and adhered to the mandate and in this year pulled off one of the most memorable shows we have had yet.

While the team was working hard on the final stages of production, we had a chance to take our annual trip to the Pan African Film Festival in mid-February (the show is at the end of the month). This year we were treated to an entertaining movie called *Whitewater*. It was a fun story about a young boy during the Civil Rights Movement who had always seen the "white only" water fountains and was reminded constantly not to drink out of those fountains. He spent much of his childhood wondering what was so special and so "different" about white water as he called it. Then he finally realized that there was no difference, and that the problem was with the people who wanted to keep us separate, not the water itself. The students in attendance had a great time of bonding as they always do with this trip. It was in essence a four-day weekend which preceded our annual Greek Week in which members of the Divine Nine Black Greek Letter Organizations came to speak with the students during the following week. It is always great to hear the guests come to speak to our students. They are often college students who are referred by my network of associates in the Divine Nine community or friends of mine, but they always enlighten and inspire our students. A highlight this year was on the day we were to welcome the sorors of Zeta Phi Beta Sorority, Incorporated from Cal State University, Los Angeles, I had to leave campus to pick up food and hurry back to greet our guests. This errand took longer than I had intended and when I returned the lunch period was almost over. However, the sorors had not only opened and held the meeting, but had the students completely engaged to the point where everyone had a great time with our guests.

They were down to earth, funny, and also gave a lot of insightful information about Greek life and their involvement in college and in their sorority. They were very inspirational to more than a few students in our BSU. This is what has come to be expected when members of the Divine Nine come to our Greek Week. As for our students, many graduate from Hamilton and later inform me that they are now a member of one of the nine organizations, and then of course they are invited back to speak future Greek Weeks.

It was now time for the show. The all-day rehearsal the day before had its usual tense moments with some people upset with last minute changes, but these things happen all the time when preparing for our show. Unlike the previous year however, the concept of this show was always very clear and never in doubt. We normally start the show with an introduction by our President and Vice President, and a general statement of what is to come. That is followed by the singing of the Black National Anthem, "Lift Ev'ry Voice and Sing." We have the audience stand and the singing of this song always gets everyone excited, primarily because of the talented singers who know the importance of getting the show off to a good start.

We have had some truly great singers open our show. However, in keeping with the idea of this being a different kind of show, the team decided to start the show in a very different way. The entire cast, (about 50 students), was dressed in black. They all stood on stage behind the curtain, those in front held signs, some were the same used in the walk-out. When the curtain opened the whole cast walked out to the very front of the stage and there were designated students who would shout out a quote. Chrystal was the first to speak, quoting Dr. Martin Luther King, Jr., "Injustice anywhere is a threat to justice everywhere!" After four more quotes the students finished by throwing their fist in the air as the lights went out. That is how this year's show, entitled "Who Will Survive in America?" began. The show took on the theme of a classroom debate. On one side of the debate were students who sought to prove that systemic racism was behind all these events we see taking place in American society. The other side held the opinion that racism was no longer a factor in the conditions in which black people find themselves. Throughout this debate there were dance routines, songs, spoken word pieces, and commercial breaks that all illustrated the feeling of the students. One of the highlights and most memorable scenes from this show was the dance scene in which there were four young men portraying four of the victims of police violence. After each one was gunned down on stage, four dancers who were their angels performed a moving and emotional dance over the "dead bodies" on stage. There were also three original spoken word pieces that brought huge applauses from the audience and were still being spoken of weeks after the show. One was called "Black Boy" written and recited by Uche and Nia, a very talented poet and writer. "I Can't Breathe was another great spoken word piece written and performed by Asha and Lewa. The last one called "Extra Extra," was written and performed by Maurice, a gifted actor in his own right who wore a trench coat and performed his piece as if giving a news flash from a street corner. The debate scenes themselves were performed brilliantly by both sides and even the commercials, which showed the disadvantages that black people have to overcome both past and present, and how with persistence we continue to succeed. I cannot stress enough the fact that these pieces were all originally written by the students. I have found it extremely important to consult with the students every year about the story they want to tell. We already know the show is going to be a highlight of the year. It is the time for

BSU to speak to the whole school and tell their story. It is also a time to attract students who are not involved in BSU. I would strongly suggest to each school that has plans to have a functioning and consistent BSU to make it a point to represent Black history or some version of the Black experience every year in a show during Black History Month. I would let nothing stop this important event. If the school doesn't usually allow events like this, which I would find hard to believe, I would push for it anyway. In addition to all the benefits to the BSU, the show is also a great source of pride for the Black students. Even during the days leading to the show we can feel the building enthusiasm within the student body. We try to be careful not to reveal what the show will be about, keeping everyone in suspense until the show begins. The important thing, again is to consult with the students, making sure that as the advisor you have criteria and parameters that the students are comfortable with. The show should never misrepresent who you are as a club, but you must know what the club stands for first. If the students can't come up with a concept for the show it is perfectly ok for them to lean on the advisor for assistance and you create the concept together. If it becomes difficult to plan the year or get students involved, there may be only one thing you can plan for the year. The show should be that one thing. You may spend the entire fall semester discussing ideas and that is alright. The few students that are present should be encouraged to tell a story, their story, or anything they want to address that involves the Black experience. The story may be controversial as this one was in 2015. I received a lot of feedback that the show was more controversial and more "aggressive" that the past shows. Some colleagues asked why the students went in that direction and my response was to have them take a step back and look at things from their perspective. "They aren't making these stories up," was my typical response. The events taking place in society are really affecting our students. We ask them to be informed and to pay attention to what's happening in the world around them. We ask them to care and to get involved whether that be speaking out about issues or registering to vote when they are old enough. This group had a message and they wanted to be heard and the show was the best way to give that message, of course it was even more effective following the walk-out. Some shows are more historically based and give a lot of interesting black facts and portrayals of historical figures, and these shows are appreciated just the same. However, there are times when students, depending on your BSU in a particular year, may want to focus more on present issues than the past. Here I must give more gratitude to the administrations that I have worked for at Hamilton who have not only allowed us to tell these stories, but have also been very supportive and even encouraging. I make sure to speak with the principal if there is a feeling that the show might be uncomfortable to some. I think this is very important to keep those lines of communication open between the BSU and the administration. Because we have that communication, our administration trusts that BSU will stay true to our principles. It is the advisor's job to make sure that in situations like this admin can trust the intentions and the integrity of the BSU. It is also important to involve the BSU President in these conversations so they know how to work with the administration, and therefore become the leaders of their peers that you are trying to develop, if that is in fact a goal of your BSU.

The bus turned the corner of Sunset and Westwood Plaza, made another quick right turn and there we were again parking and ready to take our walk toward Wilson Plaza to the steps of the Student Activities Center at UCLA where we will once again be greeted by our buddies. This was our second Buddy Day trip, but this one was going to be different from all the others. This is the first time former Hamilton BSU students were among those buddies who would be hosting us. Keara, Ameinah, Jai, and others had gone to UCLA, but none were involved with this Buddy Day trip, except for Ameinah, who was the organizer, but she had already graduated when I started the BSU. We had four former BSU students who were now in their first year at UCLA, and as we walked up to the stairs where we usually gathered outside to hear from the buddies, there they were, Camille, Donovan, Malaijah, and Iyana along with several other UCLA students, but it was so special to see our current students being greeted by their peers who were at Hamilton just a year ago. These were tenth grade students who attended the trip, but I also took Kenya and a few other 11th graders, and I also brought the students who got accepted and would be attending UCLA. In this case there was one, Chantel. I started doing this the previous year when I would take to the spring Buddy Day trip any BSU senior who had been accepted and planned to attend UCLA. It was an opportunity for them to experience this trip no longer as applicants, but now as admitted students. Before we left that year we also started a tradition to have those newly admitted students take a picture with the Bruin Bear located along the Bruin walk not far from where we congregated for lunch. It was now Chantel's turn and I was extremely happy for her. This was a student who was loved by everyone on campus. She was a great student, a dedicated friend, and a joy to be around for all. After we went through the day's activities of our students spending time with their buddies, eating lunch, watching the UCLA students gather on the stage for "Black Wednesday," the day of the week when the black students on campus either have, or take, the opportunity to showcase any activity or event on the stage along the Bruin Walk. For the students on the trip, especially those who struggle with their own self-confidence, attending UCLA, or a school like UCLA, or college in general seems tangible with trips like this. As noted earlier, they just saw many of these students last year on Hamilton's campus. After Chantel took her picture with the Bruin Bear and before well left to return to campus we met on the steps one last time for closing remarks or any final discussions. This time I asked Chantel to go down and stand with the UCLA students as they gave their remarks. She was one of them. That made her feel really special, and I also wanted that moment to symbolize for our young students that this is possible for them.

It was now time for us to host the 2015 African American Family Day. This would be our third time hosting this event which had become one of the biggest events in the district. Our BSU leaders were now being asked more and more to participate in the planning meetings and give input to make the event more appealing to students. These meetings begin about a year in advance to make sure every detail is carefully planned and every potential problem is considered. The event was to take place on April 25, 2015. Our special guests included author and radio personality Wes Hall who would be our keynote speaker, and also special guests writer, film director and produce Reginald Hudlin, and actor and producer Jay Ellis. By now about a dozen schools were actively participating in this event and the leaders of our school district would be in attendance as well. On the day of the event black families from all of the participating schools were once again welcomed to a great day of workshops, entertainment, networking, food, and inspiration from our speakers. Though this was not a BSU sponsored event, our BSU leaders were involved in its organization from the beginning, and that is in addition to all the other BSU events that we did host. A look at our BSU's activities by the end of the school year and you can see just how busy the group is during the course of an entire year. That is how a group of four hundred students can stay actively involved in our BSU because there will be opportunities for every member to participate in some event or activity that we plan, or that we are invited to. In addition to the weekly meetings and the daily camaraderie that is shown between the members there is always something, some opportunity for the students to take advantage of, and that goes even into the summer. Programs like the Vice Provost Initiative Program for Scholars (VIPS) at UCLA recruit our top black students during their tenth- grade year to participate in this highly competitive, but truly remarkable intensive college prep program, where they meet with a mentor during the school year, but spend five weeks during the summer on UCLA's campus as part of a cohort with students from other schools. This outstanding program is just part of the great outreach that I have seen from UCLA, but I am certain that colleges and universities have similar outreach efforts to attract African American high school students. These opportunities should be sought after by every BSU advisor.

May 1 is always an exciting time for me personally as it relates to our BSU because students will make their decision on where they will go to college, if they haven't already. By now I had an entire wall in my classroom filled with college acceptance letters by dozens of seniors. Uche would be attending Cal State University, Northridge in the fall. She had a tough job in following such a dynamic President in Camille, but I would say she more than met the challenge and left a mark of her own. I call 2015 the Protest Year. It was, even to this day, the most politically involved of the groups I have worked with. Not only were they politically active, they were a very close-knit group. So many of them were leaders of their own friend groups that they made being a part of BSU even cooler than it was thought to be before. Our membership would take another big jump next year and in the years to come. For example, the freshmen of that year would be the first to participate in the United Black Student Unions of California (you will read much more about this group later). This 2015 class was not as interested in leading the school, as in membership in ASB, but they did want to highlight the power of the black voice and the strength gained from the black experience, which they did a great job of demonstrating. I mentioned earlier that this group held two events that have not been attempted since they graduated. One was the Halloween Dance, but the other was their very own end of the year BSU Senior party. This was an on-campus event after lunch in our South Hall, which is adjacent to the south side of the cafeteria. They got the approval of our administration since they had finished their final exams. There was food, music, dancing of course, lots of laughter, and some very emotional send-offs between the students. It almost felt like it was already their class reunion. They truly didn't want to say good-bye to one another. I enjoyed the party with them, feeling an enormous sense of pride in this group. They were truly a family, and in many ways, it was a renaissance year, a new beginning to what had already been an amazing five years. The only thing left to do was to install next year's leadership and that came down to two extraordinary students who spent a lot of time sharpening their skills as leaders over the past few years and becoming strong voices of the class of 2016. My newly added role as Athletic Director made me even more busy than ever before but I had to make time to hold the interviews for these two dynamic young ladies. After the process was complete Dou'jae Rice would be named our BSU

President for the class of 2016 and Imani Williams would be named Vice President. Again, two of the most respected students on campus because of the way they carried themselves and the way they interacted with their peers. They were confident and they both epitomized what scholarship, leadership, and service was all about. The BSU Secretary for this next year would be none other than my own daughter Kenya. This was truly special for me to see, remembering how shy she was when she first arrived three years ago. Now she will be one of the leaders on campus. If anyone knew the inner workings of our BSU and how it should be run, it was Kenya. She had heard all the stories from years past. She had a feel for what I wanted and what changes should be made. She would bring all that knowledge to the Executive Board. I couldn't wait to get the next year started.

The Family

6
A Family Affair

One of the things I like most about BSU is the opportunity to see the leadership change hands from one year to the next. At the end of each year we begin looking for candidates for leadership roles for the next year. This usually begins after Spring Break and into the month of May. I cannot tell you how many times a student will come to me and ask how they can get more involved in BSU for the next year, or how they can get on the Executive Board for next year. What I usually see is students will sign up for BSU as freshmen, but they don't really understand what it means to be in an active high school club, so they may not get very involved. They may not attend the meetings, and if they do, they may not participate as much in the discussions or even with their attendance at the events. Because our BSU is so active and there are different committees and meetings happening all the time, the more involved you are, the more of your lunchtime you might have to give up to attend meetings. Most freshmen in my experience are not used to giving up so much of their lunchtime. Then what happens is they go through a whole school year and see all that the BSU does on campus and the field trips off campus and the fun that the students have and generate for the whole campus, then they decide to get more involved in tenth grade. They begin to attend more meetings in tenth grade and some even inquire or audition to be in the BSU show and they attend special events like Greek Week and the Yard Show, and then they have their own Buddy Day trip to UCLA in the spring, and that is usually when they begin to express a desire to get more involved. By junior year several students are usually added to the Executive Board, primarily for two reasons. One is that they have been around and are familiar enough with how the BSU works that they are ready to take on a leadership role. The other reason is that it is important to have continuity in the leadership of the BSU. I like to have underclassmen in leadership roles because I don't want to have to start all over with a whole new Executive Board each year. I can even add a third reason, and that is because the students need to know that the BSU is not for seniors only. In some cases, I have spoken with advisors at other schools who share that when the seniors graduate they have to literally start the BSU over again because there are no members, or certainly no one to step up as leaders. I cannot stress the importance of getting younger students involved as early as possible. Now the natural flow that I have described is typical of most classes, but there are those cases when you have exceptional freshmen who come to campus ready to get involved and to lead from day one. That was the case with the graduating class of 2015. That class was a very close group but they did not have that same closeness with the students who were not seniors. They were all great leaders, but the beauty of the group was their ties to one another. That is where the current leadership breaks and establishes its own identity as the 2016 board.

The students of the 2016 BSU Executive Board, led by Dou'jae Rice paid lots of attention to the class before them. They saw the protests, they enjoyed the show and they recognized the great leadership qualities in many of the leaders. They too were a group that was close, but they grew close over the years. These were not a group of students who knew each other as they entered high school. Though naturally some students did, but many of these students came from different areas and smaller charter schools. Over the course of their three years together they grew into a close-knit family, and this feeling of family would carry the BSU throughout this school year. Over Kenya's first three years of high school she was able to learn some of the advantages or should I say perks of going to a school where your parent works. This was the first time one of my children had that experience, since I had worked at a high school throughout their childhood. Some of those perks might be that when my assistants and I decide to order food, I would always get Kenya something to eat. Therefore, she didn't have to worry about bringing lunch on certain days. Also, like the other students, Kenya was issued a hall locker during her ninth-grade year. This was a locker that she never actually used because she kept her books in my classroom. Slowly I would notice, and I am sure without her approval, her friends would also use my classroom to store their books between classes. This was certainly a year in which room 508b became as popular as it had ever been. That year Kenya was my teacher's aid during first period. She had spent every school day in that room as the hangout spot during the breaks, but now it was her first period class. She did a great job helping the other students with individual work and several students grew fond of her. When the class ended each day, it was the nutrition break that followed. Immediately some students would leave to enjoy their time outside, but many would stay behind, and within minutes the room was full again with students who preferred to enjoy their break in my classroom. These were very fun and quite funny times each day. I typically stayed inside with them and engaged in whatever conversation or activity that took place. The 508B conversations became legendary. Dou'jae and Kenya were very good friends so she always came, but so did many others who just loved the atmosphere. I would sometimes sit back and watch the students get along, and then it really started to feel like they were actually my children. It also felt like, more than any of the past years, the students looked to me as not just the BSU advisor, but as a father figure. This is why, when organizing a BSU, it is extremely important to have a foundation of guiding principles and a clear mission. Leadership changes. Students change.

Even if the BSU leaders all were returning students from a year ago, they are now a year older, and there will still be changes. There were very distinct differences between the class of 2014, 2015, and 2016 at Hamilton High. The class of 2014 leadership focused on inclusion, love, and freedom of expression, all in the atmosphere of social justice, but they didn't focus on the *fight*, they focused on the *love*. The class of 2015 took that freedom of expression and were much more forceful and vocal about the demand for justice. They focused on the fight at hand and collectively spoke out about the desire and the need to keep fighting. The class of 2016 now, having experienced the same look at social justice issues, and feeling the same need to express themselves focused on their strength and ability to address these issues by emphasizing black excellence, their black excellence. This was the class that fought back by beating and breaking the stereotypes, proving that they can excel in any situation and still love one other. The focus was not on the proverbial "them," it was on us. "What are *we* going to do to show how great *we* are? How can *we* help each other and hold each other accountable to a standard of greatness?" Without a solid foundation, a clear mission, and guiding principles, who are you as a BSU? I suggest to you that you will be reinventing the club every year exactly because of the dynamic students who will lead your group. However, with that solid foundation, your BSU will continue to remain strong each year, and at the same time, your students will have the impact that they hope to have. What does this look like? Let's take a close look at this class of 2016.

The first activity of the year was the annual Back-to-School Night and our fundraising chair, Jaimee, got us going by informing us that her dad owns a barbecue restaurant. She volunteered to ask him about supplying barbecue dinners for us to sell for the event, to which he said yes. In the past, I had gone and bought chicken wings or hot links from a local grocery store. This time we would be selling actual dinners complete with beans and potato salad. The dinners were a huge success as parents stopped by the table to support, and to have a good dinner for the night. In some cases it was the students bringing the parents over, but mostly the parents came on their own. We sold all the dinners we had and made lots of money that night. We helped promote a black-owned business, raised money for our club, and got students and parents excited about our BSU. It was a great way to start the year. Serving the Hamilton family and community would be another theme all year. The service mentality of this year's BSU was prevalent in each activity.

This was also a year of many changes. We were transitioning to a new Principal, as Mr. Garcia, who had been extremely supportive of our BSU over the years had left to take another position. Before leaving however, he had appointed myself and another teacher, Ms. Cooley, as the co-Athletic Directors of the school last spring. This new role was yet another very time-consuming position, and obviously one that would challenge and conflict with my responsibility as BSU advisor. Nevertheless, I was still very excited about the new position because athletics was still a passion of mine and this gave me an opportunity to work in athletics from a different perspective other than as a coach. I dove into the position last spring near the end of the school year as track and field season was finishing. My plan was to devote the summer to getting to know our football coaching staff, the players, and how the program was run. Football is the sport that has the most students, requires the most money to run, and it is the most popular sport that takes place at the beginning of the school year. My objective was to make sure that our football program was ready to go from day one of the school year, especially since we had won the L.A.

City Championship the previous season. Many of our students on the football team were also in our BSU, which was also the case with basketball and many other sports. Another objective was to, whenever possible, blend athletics and the athletes into BSU activities and vice versa. I would make sure BSU played some role in athletic events and have the programs work together as much as possible. For example, during Club Rush which was only weeks after Back to School Night, BSU had the usual location near the area where the football team hung out during nutrition and lunch, a very popular spot already. This time the students recruited members of the football team to help promote the club, and it was also a great way for them to get to know the student body and vice versa, bringing more attention and popularity to the program, which would bring more people out to the games each Friday. Kenya, being a member of the volleyball team, which also had BSU members also helped out and Club Rush became an even bigger event because of this participation by the athletes as well. The turnout was tremendous and the membership of our BSU grew to over 450 signed up members. Once again, the objective for each of them was to participate and contribute when they could, benefit whenever possible, but represent always.

We continued on with our weekly meetings in my classroom and these meetings were even more important to me at this time because I was so busy during the week with my many other responsibilities. My role as Athletic Director kept me extremely busy even during lunch time. I dedicated Wednesdays, however, to BSU meetings. The rest of the days I had to keep up with the athletic paperwork and make sure all the athletes were eligible. There seemed to always be issues of an athlete needing some required form or documentation to make sure they were eligible. This was especially the case with the football team. There were so many more students to monitor, and that's not including students who were transfers waiting to be eligible for competition. In a typical football season there may be a student who transferred to the school, but has to wait for a certain amount of days before practicing or competing. I found myself constantly checking with the athletics office in our district to make sure a particular athlete was cleared, and believe me, the players and the coaches made sure to check with me regularly. During the time I spent with our football program I learned that we had at least two students who were being recruited to play college football. We had been selected that season to play one of our Friday football games on a Saturday as the Game of the Week in the city of Los Angeles. This game would be played at the Los Angeles Coliseum where we won the championship game last season. The game of the week would be against Los Angeles High School, not exactly a rival, but a program that had emerged as one of the best teams in the city that season. As Athletic Director, I had to make sure all the logistics were taken care of by coordinating with the city athletics office as we were the home team. As BSU advisor, however, I could not overlook the great opportunity this was for our BSU students who were on the team. As advisors, we should all be looking to support our BSU students in the other areas of interest they may have. We are mentors to our students and therefore we should take an interest in everything they do when we can. Because of my athletic background and my role as Athletic Director it was a little easier for me to support our student-athletes. The game was very exciting and came down to the last seconds to determine a winner. With less than a minute to play and Hamilton winning by five points, LA High was down to its last play at midfield. It was fourth down and about 12 yards to go for a first down. All we had to do was stop them on this play and we would win the game in front of a huge crowd at the Coliseum, who had been treated to a great game already. When LA snapped the ball their quarterback found himself under a huge rush by one of our highly recruited athletes Emanuel Joseph. Under heavy pressure the quarterback scrambles to his right and seemingly out of desperation throws the ball back to his left where their wide receiver had come back as an emergency target. The wide receiver caught the pass and eluded our defensive back and was off to the races to the end zone. We couldn't catch him from behind. Touchdown. Fortunately, there was still enough time for our other top recruit, quarterback Armani Rogers to drive the team downfield and get us in position to score a touchdown and win the game. He did just that. However, with just seconds left and our last play of the game, Armani's pass sailed too high over our receiver's head and was intercepted in the back of the end zone. Game over. We played a great game and our BSU students were outstanding. It was at that point I began to think of how we could honor our student-athletes once the season was over. Ideally, the Athletic Director, the administration, the student body and the coaches would work together to honor the student-athletes who had extraordinary seasons. These are the ones you might see giving press conferences announcing where they intend to play at the collegiate level. Since we had an interim principal, and I was new to the AD position and had not worked with the student body very much, I knew there would be no press conference or any celebration on that scale. The coaches were going to have their annual banquet, but I wanted to do something as well. When it was signing day for the football players, I decided to make our BSU meeting a celebration of their peers by honoring the scholarship athletes. There were no news cameras, however, but we did have a few speeches. The two football players, Armani and Emanuel brought their hats and placed them on the table before them. Armani's cap read UNLV, University of Nevada Las Vegas, and Emanuel's cap read New Mexico, as he would be headed to Albuquerque to play at the University of New Mexico. The head coach was there as well as about fifty BSU students. I explained to the gathering the importance of the meeting and honoring our athletes. I wanted them to understand that nothing should stop us from celebrating our own students and our own accomplishments. The idea of supporting one another in our conduct and in our discourse has been a constant message of mine to our BSU. I have long held the belief that we, as black youth, tear each other down way too much. It happened many years ago when I was in high school, and I saw the same thing on campus and in my classroom as a teacher. It may be for a good laugh in the moment, but so much of those punchlines are carried home, internalized, and then manifest later in all types of attention-seeking and at-risk behaviors. Those jokes can often ruin a child's self-esteem especially when there is no positive affirmation to balance the onslaught of negativity endured during those teenage years. In my own way, I was trying to get our students to do more affirming, encouraging, and supporting one another, not just the student-athletes, but with all of their peers, starting with their BSU brothers and sisters. The BSU leaders of this class did a great job of carrying that message to their peers. I would sit in my classroom and hear the conversations when students were expressing their support for one another. Additionally, I modeled this whenever I could. After a while you could feel the tone changing ever so subtly where it became a little more common to hear the affirmations.

We attended our annual Buddy Day trip to UCLA in November and of course by this time all the seniors had begun applying to colleges across the country. This process always takes our seniors, mine and yours, on an emotional rollercoaster. I always try to remind the underclassmen to pay attention to the stress the seniors come under during college application season. However, this process always seems to catch the seniors off guard and totally unprepared. There is often pressure from home to start looking at colleges, a conversation that starts to sneak into the daily discourse among peers. What that looks like at school when I see the students is a look of complete confusion. I might ask, "Have you talked to your counselor, or the college counselor?" "I did but...Mr. Turner I don't what I'm doing. I need help," which pretty much captures the usual response. Another role of the advisor is to help guide the students through this process. You may or may not have the position of counselor on your campus, but it really doesn't matter. You are the one they trust. You are the one they feel they can be vulnerable with because they are very vulnerable. They may not need you to come up with all the answers, at least not yet; they are looking for help formulating the questions. They don't know what they don't know. This is precisely why trips like the Buddy Day trip are necessary. Where ever you are in the country, you are in proximity to some college or university where the students can learn to navigate this process. When our students are on UCLA's campus they are gaining valuable information that helps them with this process. There is always a time to ask questions of the panel, and if the students don't ask for themselves, I usually ask questions that I know they want to, but are afraid to, or at least hadn't thought of, but need to know the answers to. For example, there is a call for any questions by the panel of college students, and after a few seconds of silence, seeing that no one will ask a question, I might get it started by asking, "What made you decide to attend UCLA instead of going to an HBCU?" This is a question that students wrestle with when it comes to choosing a college. I know that because I seek out every senior in our BSU, (or they seek me out), every year and have these conversations. I usually begin asking them these types of questions during the spring of their junior year. I try to ease the stress I know they are going to experience when the time comes. There is choosing a school, applying to the schools of choice, applying for financial aid and scholarships, the

149

ever-stressful waiting game, and then finally making the decision. Did I mention applying for scholarships? That is an ongoing process. They are doing all this while still trying to keep grades up, and then of course the senior activities like prom, and if they're in a club like our BSU, they are even more busy. I fail to mention whatever might be going on at home. The greatest service we can do for our students is walk them through this process from beginning to end. This year was especially interesting in this regard because it was now Kenya's turn. She applied to UCLA as did Dou'jae. We had several students apply to UCLA as usual. During the senior trip, once again we were greeted by former Hamilton BSU students who were now Yankee Bruins. Former President Camille was there as was Malaijah and Donovan, but this time Chantel had joined them. It was great to see her now as a UCLA student, quite naturally I was very proud. The trip made those students who did apply much more excited about the possibility of getting accepted.

This year we were also invited to Cal State Northridge for their Harambee Conference, making this our second college visit of the year, and one of those events that we had not planned for, but were able to take advantage of. This conference was unlike Buddy Day as there were many schools present and the day's activities were held in their University Student Union, until the groups were divided and escorted on campus tours. School representatives gave very good presentations on all the things that CSUN had to offer. The prevailing sentiment at Hamilton at that time was students didn't want to go to Northridge because they felt that too many Hamilton students go there, and they wanted a different experience. That sentiment changed for the students who went on that field trip. That was totally due to exposure to the campus and what they were able to see while being there. In Los Angeles, any given high school may have up to a dozen universities within less than an hour drive from the high school. I encourage BSU advisors to visit and develop ongoing relationships with many of these universities. So much of what you might want to do with your BSU is being done, or can be assisted at the local college or university.

This year we were presented with yet another opportunity that wasn't expected. I received an email invitation from the California Legislative Black Caucus. They were inviting high schools to come to an event in Century City, a fifteen-minute bus ride from Hamilton High School. This was an opportunity to see and learn how elected officials carried out their duties while in office. It was sort of a peek into the daily activities of politicians, and of course by this time we were less than a year from a very important presidential election coming in November 2016. The campaigns of Hillary Clinton and Donald Trump were in full swing so this was an important event to be a part of, so I gladly accepted the invitation. When we arrived at the location it was great to see colleagues from other schools, and also for so many of my students to see friends from other schools as well. The session began with the greetings from the officials and an acknowledgement of the schools present, probably ten schools were there. The Hamilton contingent was about 20 BSU students, who all were asked to come with professional attire. It was nice to see so many of my students on this trip, dressed in their business attire, and eager to see how the day would unfold. This is where this class was at their best. They thrived in situations where they could show their intelligence. The students were given a quick lesson on how bills are introduced, debated, and finally passed or voted down in the legislature. The large group of students was divided into two smaller groups. The two groups were given a proposed bill and asked to each take a side arguing for or against the bill. Each side had to caucus and then choose a spokesperson for the group who would debate the other side. I was extremely proud to see that in each of the two groups one of my BSU students was selected to debate the issue. On one side of the debate was Dou'jae, and on the other side was our Vice President, Imani. I had the pleasure of hearing these two extremely intelligent young ladies speak on issues every day. It was now time for others to hear them articulate their respective positions. The two went back and forth, each receiving verbal affirmation from their respective sides until it was time to stop the debate and cast the votes. The officials declared that the bill would become law based on the votes, and congratulated both the speakers as well as the entire group of students. After a light lunch, we returned back to school. Whenever possible, we always go to a room on campus and debrief upon returning from a field trip. We almost always arrive back to campus with at least 30 minutes left in the school day. I keep the students with me until the dismissal bell rings. During that debriefing time it is always enlightening to hear what the students thought about the trip, what they learned, what they liked, or didn't like. This time of reflection often helps students process what happened and then helps them with important decisions.

When we return to school from Christmas vacation, we are typically in show mode from then until the end of February. Our two show directors, Maurice and Lewa, happened to both be outstanding actors and therefore were cast in productions in the music academy, which took a lot of their time. Kenya and I spent a lot time talking about show topics and I reached into my show bag as it were, and came across an idea that I thought would be different from the past two shows and more similar to the ones before. This would be more of a historical dive into an aspect of black history that had not been talked about much, and certainly not taught about in history classes, but would definitely be educational. The idea was to take a look at the millions of Africans who were brought to America as slaves, but not those who ended up in North America. I thought a great show would be to focus on those who were brought to South America. I thought it would be a great idea to present to our audience the history of places like Haiti, Brazil, and many Caribbean and South American countries. We would focus on the Africans who, over the years, were very influential in that part of the world including Latin America all the way to Los Angeles. The show would be very educational as always, but it would also include some of the entertainment pieces from those countries. When I informed the board of the theme of the show, they were very excited. It was not just that this theme had not been done before, but they knew the show would feature lots of new ideas even with the entertainment. We were all very excited to get started. We got off to a very late start in planning the show this particular year. Our goal is to always have a good sense of what we want to do by Thanksgiving. That gives us about three months to write, hold auditions, and cast the show. However, this year we were writing the show literally until the night before. The problem was our show was scheduled to last seventy minutes, but when the show was written and all the acts were in place including dances and everything else, the show was only about 45 minutes. Therefore, we needed to add about 25 more minutes of content to the show. The good thing was there was so much content in terms of Africans who had influenced that part of the world. We simply had to do more research. The challenging thing was to find a way to present the information to our audience. It was not just about reading facts, but we wanted the delivery to be entertaining. That meant some of the pieces needed to be in the form of spoken word, some had to be acted out, and still others performed as dance pieces. As we gathered the performers who were going to be needed to pull this off, I can remember on more than one occasion one of our dancers' reassuring words, "I got you Mr. Turner." Darnita was an extraordinary dancer and had the ability to pull the dancers together and create something out of seemingly nothing. I credit this to the great working relationship I have with Ms. Douglas, and the amazing job she does with her dancers. They simply are always ready. The day before the show was intense and the level of focus was on high. People were trying to learn lines they were just given, and to many, it seemed like we weren't going to be ready. All hands were on deck as even Kenya was helping some learn lines. I had even written a piece that was to be read by one of our amazing actors named Robert, who fortunately was very skilled in performing and could learn lines very quickly. My piece was a poem to be read as Toussaint L'Overture, who faught against the French for Haitian independence. Not to my anyone's surprise, Robert nailed it. The next day during the show, the audience was introduced to ancient Kings and Queens of Africa, performed by our students as they strolled from the back of the auditorium to the sounds of "Tutu" by Myles Davis performed by jazz bass legend Marcus Miller. I wish Marcus was there, but this was part of our sound track. They were treated to great spoken word pieces and also a wonderful Capoeira dance by Darnita and another great dancer, Camia. There was a Caribbean dance by several of our dancers that the audience really enjoyed, and then there was the finale, a wonderfully choreographed dance by Naiya to Rihanna's "Work." What happened during that routine was truly amazing. While the dancers were performing, the music stopped. However, the dancers continued to dance as if the music was still playing and did not miss a beat. The audience showed their appreciation with a loud applause before they could even finish. We did the show four times and unfortunately, we had problems with the sound system each time. That wasn't the only problem that we had. Days after the show it was brought to my attention that there were Egyptian students at school who were offended, even upset, that we mentioned the Kings and Queens of Egypt during the part of the show that focused on African Kings and Queens. No one asked to speak to me about it. It was just brought to my attention by students. I was actually waiting for someone to come to me so we could discuss the situation, but no one came. As far as I knew, we were accurate in our presentation, but obviously those in that community disagreed. In hindsight, much later I realized I should have gone to them to seek clarification about where they think we were wrong, but at the time I figured that someone would at least want to meet with me to discuss. It has always been important to me to make sure the shows we produce are accurate, and if they offend anyone I am always open to learn where and how we could do better. Some of the shows tackle very sensitive issues and will undoubtedly make some feel uncomfortable. When telling stories that are unique to black people in America, the advisor and the BSU must be true to the history and at the same time be prepared with factual information to support the position. If the situation arises you must also be willing to discuss with other groups in a constructive conversation, much like I had to the year before when the show took a raw look at police brutality. The truth is that there are stories to tell and this is a great way to tell them and to share how those stories make the students feel. I can't overstate the importance of taking advantage of this platform.

Our annual Greek Week event as well as our trip to the Pan African Film Festival always bring the students together as great bonding events, which are needed to help prepare for the show. The movie we were able to see this particular year was *Mandela*. It was not only a great time to be together, but also provided for a great discussion in our debrief when we returned. The movie, which looked at the political climate in South Africa and the life of Nelson Mandela was also important for the students to see in light of the fact that the election of our President was to be held later in November. The students had been paying lots of attention to the campaigns of Hilary Clinton and Donald Trump and were getting more interested, and anxious, about the election. The subject of the campaigns came up in more than a few of our BSU meetings during the Spring of 2016, but there was still more activities and events planned for the year, so most of the time left in the school year was spent on making sure our annual African American Family Day, which we scheduled for fall 2016, and Buddy Day went well, and that we had a good send off for our seniors. In preparation for Family Day, Ms. Monroe and the organizing team wanted to have an evening meeting/dinner at Hamilton in our library to bring together the student leaders of the BSUs involved in the event. The dinner turned out really nice and the students got a chance to network and share with each other what was going on with the respective BSU's. We had a guest speaker, Dr. Brenda Manuel, who shared some of the opportunities available for schools and for students. One of those opportunities was called the United Black Student Unions of California, or the UBSUC. She mentioned that it was this organization that consisted of BSU's from throughout the state of California and that they have this annual state convention that was coming up. The state convention is when all the BSU's get together for a weekend of activities like workshops, a college tour, entertainment, and motivational speakers. I had never heard of this organization, but the more I listened to Dr. Manuel, the more I realized that this was something I needed to know about. It was too late for us to attend the convention this year, but I thought that I would do my research and possibly take students to the convention the following year. On our second Buddy Day trip, in addition to the 10th graders, we got to take three seniors who had been admitted. Dou'jae had been admitted and so had Jolen and Louis. These were two young men who were great representatives of our BSU. Jolen served as our

Historian, but Louis did not hold any office on our Executive Board. He was however a great student, and an outstanding basketball player who had just competed in four straight city championship games with our team. As is now a tradition, they took their picture with the Bruin Bear near the Wooden Center during this trip. Because Chantel was so popular among her peers at Hamilton, many students chose to shadow her that day. It was great to see because the alumni are a big part of our family and now we had reached a point where many BSU alumni were attending several local universities and also those across the country.

Observing all the Buddy Day and Family Day activities, and having been impacted by past leaders like Camille, who was also a buddy on that wonderful trip, was an 11th grader who I had allowed to attend. This is the same student who had shared with me that she had wanted to be BSU President since the sixth grade. It was now time for her to submit her application as did a few others. We held the interviews during lunchtime in room 510, next door to my room. All the students were given their score sheets with the questions to ask and evaluate. Our biggest BSU supporter, Ms. Monroe was present as well. After interviewing the three candidates who had made it to that stage in the process, Aretha Bernard would in fact emerge as the selection for BSU President for the class of 2017. This had been years in the making and she accomplished just what she set out to do. In the next chapter, you will find that that is what Aretha does. She sets her mind to accomplish something and she focuses in on that goal, and she makes it happen. Over the course of her three years at Hamilton we had grown very close, and now she was BSU President. I would be able to work with her throughout her senior year. What I did not anticipate was that I would learn much more from her than she would from me.

7

A Time of Self-Reflection

The 2016-17 school year brought about many changes for me personally and for our BSU. The first change met me during the summer before school started as I was going for my not-so-regular walk around Circle Park in my Inglewood neighborhood. I received a call from our new Principal Brenda Pensamiento asking me if I would be interested in a new position outside the class titled Intervention Coordinator. She knew I was interested in advancing in my career one day becoming an administrator, and that this position would help me reach that goal. I was obviously very flattered to be considered the right person for the job, and I began to think about how I could be effective in this new role. Then I realized it would mean giving up my position as Athletic Director. I had only spent one year as AD but I grew to really like that side of athletics and wanted to continue. That was the hardest part of the decision once I was assured I could continue as BSU advisor. I knew that I would have an office, and I would have more control of my movement around campus, not being confined to a classroom anymore. I would not have as much control of my time though, as now I would be servicing the entire school, and not just working with the students in my classroom, so I had to be ready to work with students any time during the day. When I accepted the position, I was confident that I made the right decision. It was time. I needed this change. Now, how would it affect the BSU? The first, and most notable change was that there was not a hangout spot anymore. For years 508B had been our home. We had our meeting place in another room, but that was different. That was somebody else's space. During our lunch and nutrition breaks now I was outside on supervision duty, and therefore I could not just sit and talk and share those laughs with the BSU students like we did before. The relationships I had with the group were still strong, but the time we spent together was not like it was before and that is something that took getting used to. The relationships that we established in BSU grew the way they did because we were able to spend so much time together, and now that was much more difficult to do without a home base. I did like the fact that we had a strong Executive Board like we always seem to have, led by Aretha and a student who came on strong at the end of last year and had established herself as a strong leader, a clear thinker, and an excellent communicator. Nijah Pine won the position of Vice President, and the two of them worked really well together. The Executive Board was filled with students who I had seen become more involved each year they were there. These were students with strong personalities, and this would prove necessary for the kind of year that was in store. We usually have our Executive Board established before school starts except for the addition of our ninth-grade reps, and they aren't added until school begins, unless something happens before, like this year. While on campus helping with early registration an alumnus from a couple years ago named Faith, got my attention and introduced me to her younger brother, Myles, who was there registering in his first year of high school. I was extremely impressed with Myles' maturity and thought he would be an excellent addition, so I made him a member of the Executive Board on the spot. I'm not even sure if I gave him a choice. Myles' first assignment was to bring to the board a fellow freshman he thought would be another great addition and, shortly after the semester began, he introduced me to Trevious, one of his good friends. Knowing how much I wanted to have more young men active in BSU and in leadership roles, I thought this would be perfect. Our Executive Board was now set. Our Secretary was a very sweet and dedicated student named Promise. Alanna, who had proved to be very consistent and trustworthy, was our Treasurer. She would work closely with Jazmine, who was our Financial Secretary, and spent a lot of time in 508b over the years. The committee chairs were all outstanding leaders in their own right and were a major reason for the large turnout we would see for Club Rush. The trio of Summer, Naiya, and Francis worked together as our Black History Program production team. Summer and Naiya were two extremely talented dancers and Francis was "Mr. Hamilton," a foundational piece of the Hamilton High School culture. The Community Service Committee was led by Carlyn, a total class act. Our Fundraising Committee chair was Mica who was totally committed to BSU, and the wonderful and dedicated Camia was our Social Activities Committee chair. An outstanding student, athlete, and young man named Matthew served as our Historian. The grade level representatives need to be mentioned here because many of them would have a huge impact on our BSU as a result of the role they played as reps. Representing the eleventh grade was Destiny and Samantha. The tenth-grade reps were Aliah and Elisha, and you have already been introduced to the ninth-grade reps. They are an example of why I continue to emphasize getting young students involved in your BSU.

We had to immediately get ready for Club Rush and African American Family Day which was scheduled for October. This was our busiest Club Rush in all my years as BSU advisor up to that date. The BSU leaders and many of the more involved students this year were some of the most popular, most liked, and most respected students on campus. And as usual we had my friend, and our partner, Nicole from Stepping In The Right Direction Black College Tours right there next to us. After Club Rush when all the sign-up sheets were totaled we had reached 450 students as our official membership. Soon that year, the school would see the power of such a large group of committed young people.

It is no secret that when we have our BSU meetings, especially the first one, I tend to talk a lot. Though I am much better now, (actually no I'm not), I am sure it was a problem then. As is our tradition, we met in the auditorium and there was a large crowd. The students got to meet the new leaders on the Executive Board, and it was a great opportunity to get everyone excited about African American Family Day. This Family Day would be the last one hosted at Hamilton High School and we wanted it to be every bit as special as the others. It had been a year in the making. We had gotten the student leaders from local schools together for a dinner last spring. This year there was a gathering at UCLA where I took Aretha and Nijah to meet with other leaders again for an inspirational message of leadership and black excellence from Mandla Kayise, the original Yankee Bruin. His words helped prepare all the students present for a great showing of leadership and pride of self and culture at Family Day. The Student Conference part of the itinerary was hosted by actor Jay Ellis who came back to be with the young people a second time. I was extremely proud of all the young people who shared their talents with the audience, which consisted mostly of their peers and also parents and educators. I have to say though that I was completely blown away by the performance of the Hamilton Dance Team. I had seen them perform many times obviously, but I think this was the best I had seen them to that point. I am still looking for someone who has that video, the still shots don't do it justice. There were also other great dance performances, spoken word pieces, singers, and musicians from local schools. A panel of college students who had been members of local BSU's in high school, spoke of their past BSU as well as their current college experience, and of course Hamilton was represented on the panel, by none other than Chantel, now in her second year at UCLA. Aretha, like those before her as President of the host BSU, served as co-MC of the event and did a fantastic job. To cap off the event, there was an outstanding and well attended college fair and lunch following the Student Conference. When that wonderful Saturday afternoon was over and all the preparation from the past year that went into it was finally complete, I had to thank Ms. Monroe, Ms. Henry, and Mitzi on behalf of the hundreds of BSU students that were positively impacted over the years we hosted African American Family Day.

After Family Day I would have my first chance to attend and take students to the Young Men's Leadership Conference. This is a LAUSD sponsored conference specifically organized to motivate young men for current and future success. There are guest speakers, workshops, a panel of professional men from various careers, entertainment, and lunch. It is a full day of excitement and learning for the young men. For this event, I decided to take ninth grade young men. It was important to me that ninth graders have some of their own experiences as members of the BSU. Ezekiel, Calvin, Quintin, Benjamin, Darnell, and DJ were a few of the young men I took on this trip along with the ninth-grade rep, Myles. Because this event takes place on a Saturday, it requires more coordination and communication with the parents than a field trip during the school day, and this is how I began to get to know parents of my BSU students. I would take students on these Saturday trips, and as you will see later, weekend trips. Pretty soon I would have dozens of parents' contacts in my cell phone and would remain in communication with them regarding any issues with which they needed my help. Calvin's mother, Ms. Black, became a very important resource for our BSU through our communications. These relationships with parents are critical to the formation and development of a BSU.

The attention of everyone on campus would quickly turn over the next few weeks to the Presidential election of 2016. I spent that evening watching the election with Kenya as she was in her freshman dorm at UC Riverside. The BSU students, like many throughout the country, had paid lots of attention to the campaigns of the candidates and, though only few were actually voting age, clearly in their mind they had a favorite. We had many conversations in meetings about the debates or other key moments leading up to the election. It was important to me that in our meetings everyone's opinion was to be heard and respected whether you agreed or disagreed. That is the same way we approached every conversation. To the students' credit they did a good job of listening to one another and there was never a problem in our meetings over political opinions. However, on election night, when the winner was declared, there was feeling of sadness and confusion that came over the students and you could see it the next day. It was our usual meeting day, Wednesday, and we had a turnout bigger than any meeting I can remember that wasn't the first meeting of the year. There was standing room only which means there was probably at least a hundred students present. This is where the advisor has to have the ability to facilitate a conversation and keep the emotions from taking over. I wanted to give as many students a chance to speak as I could. It was extremely important for them to be able to express themselves in this space with their peers. These were students who were involved in their school community, who cared about their city, and the country, and I could see the concern in their eyes, and hear it in their voices. I was especially proud of the optimism that came from our Fundraising Chair Mica. All these students had a tremendous amount of respect for each other, so when one spoke, they all listened. In the midst of much despair in the room Mica steps up to speak and reminds the students that, "we will get through this just like every other election and past President our parents and ancestors had to endure because it's in our DNA." I stood back and just admired how special this group was. It touched my heart to hear a student remind her peers what's "in our DNA." Because she was absolutely right. I have encouraged, and even challenged, many times to our BSU to look back at our ancestors and study the history of our people and draw strength from those who came before them. That meeting remains one of my proudest moments as BSU advisor at Hamilton because of the resolve and the commitment of the students to take ownership of their progress and to take care of each other. As I think back, that meeting was probably the beginning of what would later be the self-actualization of our BSU.

While the emotions were high on campus, and you could feel the cloud of uneasiness hovering over the city, we still managed to take our annual senior Buddy Day trip to UCLA. That fall we were greeted by former Yankees Dou'jae and Jolen, who were now first year Bruins and among the buddies our students would shadow. The college application season was now upon the seniors and the recent election was one more thing that waged war on the students' concentration, so this trip provided a break and a reminder for the students to keep pushing and the inspiration they drew from the UCLA students was even more critical than it had been in recent years. Back on campus it was not surprising to learn that plans were being made for a student walk-out in protest of the plans of the new President to build a wall on the U.S./Mexico border, and the discourse that pervaded the news about Mexican students, and Mexican people in general. There was real fear felt by many of our students that they or their families and friends would be deported. There was also the tone of the national conversation that made those students feel targeted at best, and worthless at the least. It was real concern to our BSU students as well. Many of the Latino Student Organization, (LaSO), students and other Mexican American students were friends and some even members of the BSU. They needed the support of their fellow students, so when I heard plans of the walk-out it just confirmed what I knew about our students, what I had seen over the years when there is a cause. Our BSU not only stood with their Mexican brothers and sisters but helped organize and lead the walk-out. Several student groups came to join, and by the time the event took place, thousands of students participated. The Hamilton community had come together once again. The students crowded the walkway in front of campus out to Robertson Blvd. and in either direction. It was clear that this meant a lot to them. Occasionally in past walk-outs and rallies, there were those who participated only to get out of class, and that was evident by the usual horseplay, but not this time. I could see in their eyes the seriousness of the moment. It was as though, just like in our BSU meeting, the students felt a responsibility for one another, and it was beautiful. You could see the signs they had written, and if you couldn't, you could certainly hear Aretha on the bullhorn leading the chant, "No walls, no gates, no bullies, no hate!" This is what it looks like when students feel empowered. They often show us exactly what we are always asking for, which is for them to be responsible, respectful, informed, and motivated individuals who want to make a difference, not only in their own lives, but also for society at large. The BSU is a great place to empower our black students to first, be informed, and then get involved in causes they find important. I tell our students to sign up, show up, speak up, and stand up. When we, and I mean educators, but particularly advisors, do not empower our students we risk losing their voice, their passion, their creativity, and even their motivation. I learned that important lesson this year.

After a very busy fall semester we were in BSU Show mode once again and the creative directors were meeting to decide on a theme once again when something happened that had never happened before. Aretha wanted the theme of the show to focus on mental health in the black community, and the directors had a completely different idea for the show, and they could not come to an agreement. I met with both sides and they felt strongly about their positions. My opinion was that while we could certainly make mental health a part of the show and incorporate it into a larger concept, I could not see making it the theme of the entire show. Remember, since her freshman year, she had seen the President very much involved with the show from beginning to end. It had come to be the President's show in many ways, so when it felt like she wouldn't have a say in the direction of the show, she was hurt and understandably so. This is where the three years that we spent together prior to her senior year came to be so important because our relationship would be tested over the next few weeks.

We would proceed with the show idea of the "Untold Story of Black Excellence." In this show, we would highlight figures in black history who the students felt had not been given enough credit for their contributions, or who at least were not known on a wide scale for their work. The concept was there was a family watching television, and the parents were educating their children about the older generation of successful black people, but also learning from the children about the current black people who were also very influential figures. The show concluded with a tribute to Don

Cornelius, and you know there was a Soul Train line at the end. It proved to be enlightening and educational, but also a very entertaining show and the audience really enjoyed themselves and the talent of their peers. Our annual February activities prior to the show continued as usual. The Greek Week guests had always consisted of associates of mine and also parents or relatives of our students. Some of the guests were even Hamilton alumni who attended before I was there. I wanted the alumni, even the older alumni, to feel proud of what their school has been able to accomplish with the BSU. Over the years we have had a consistent presence at our Greek Week event from the sorors of Alpha Kappa Alpha, Delta Sigma Theta, Zeta Phi Beta, and Sigma Gamma Rho sororities as well as the men of Alpha Phi Alpha, Kappa Alpha Psi, Omega Psi Phi, and Phi Beta Sigma fraternities. I especially enjoy when my colleagues at Hamilton from the Greek community come as guest speakers representing their organizations. My fraternity brother, Coach Brown, our boys basketball coach is always faithful in this regard as is Ms. Cooley, our wonderful Math teacher and member of Delta Sigma Theta Sorority, Inc. Mr. Tolson, a new faculty member, and former BSU student of mine always represents his brothers of Omega Psi Phi Fraternity, Inc. This not only shows their support for our BSU, but it also helps the students see these teachers in a completely different light. Our Pan African Film Festival trip this year was another great experience as this time we got to see *Hidden Figures*, the inspirational movie about three African American women who worked for NASA in the 1960's, including Katherine Johnson, the first African American woman to work as a NASA scientist. In our conversation about the movie in a subsequent meeting, we had what I thought was a good dialogue about the impact of those women, and what we can learn from their example. When the meeting was over and it was time to go to class, I noticed that Aretha was in a sort of somber mood. As we walked to her class I asked her what was wrong, and she responded with something that took me by surprise, but I needed to hear. She said to me, "You don't empower me." I asked her what she meant by that and she basically reminded me as President she was supposed to be leading the BSU, and I hadn't given her the confidence and authority necessary to do so. Although outwardly I was trying to process what she was saying, inwardly I knew she was right. I thought about the meeting that had just ended, that I basically ran and facilitated. That is what *she* should have been doing, but there I was in the way. She got to her class and I could not stop thinking about what she said. I had to take a big step backward and remember that I am the advisor of the BSU, but it is *their* club. Over these seven years we had reached a point where my colleagues, the administration, and students alike saw me as the creator and undisputed leader of the BSU. All questions, comments, and concerns were brought to me, and I accepted that as the reality on our campus. The truth is the President and the leaders of the BSU should be able to answer any question that is brought to me. Ideas, plans, and decisions are all discussed together so they should be known to all the leaders. I had taken way more control and more space in the position of leader than I should have, and this was completely true, and my fault. The problem was, giving up the control was not easy at that time because we were nearing that period when seniors naturally fall back and focus on their senior activities. This is when I typically step in and usher the transitioning leaders into place. I felt our relationship was tested because more than anything Aretha deserved to have a strong finish to her senior year, and a positive overall high school experience. I did not want to be the reason she didn't, and I thought I might be. After a while she probably didn't feel like she could lead the group because I had been doing that, and before long the college acceptance season was here and that was the main concern. Aretha had neither heard from, nor been accepted at schools she was applying to and began to have serious doubts, or at least concerns about her next move. I am so thankful for our relationship because that became the focus of our conversations, her future. She contemplated going to junior college, which I knew she didn't really want to do. That is why I was so excited, almost moved to tears, when she came and said to me in her high-pitched soprano voice, "Tell me why I just got a scholarship to Clark Atlanta University." Against the discouragement from the application process, and my not empowering her to be the leader that we both knew she was, and all the doubts about leading her peers, there was now this. No one deserved this more than Aretha, and I am forever grateful for the lesson she taught me. Because of her I am much better in my role as BSU advisor. The lesson here for any advisor is to remember to teach and advise the students, but let them lead. We must teach them how to lead in some cases, and we can make suggestions and consult with them, and bring all sorts of ideas to the table, but let the leaders lead. And we can also create a culture where those not in leadership roles understand and respect those who are. Let the students know that you are always looking for the next leaders of your BSU. Get them excited about their own opportunities to lead their peers and they will respect the officers before them. This was not my best year as advisor, but I would become much better and more aware later because of Aretha, and we would stay in touch as she went on to do great things at Clark Atlanta.

A year had passed now and I had been able to remain in contact with Ms. Washington, the representative of the United Black Student Unions of California (UBSUC). It was time for the annual spring convention which this year would take place in Los Angeles. I found out that each year this convention rotates between the Southern, Central, and Northern regions of California. This year was the South's turn. The host university was Loyola Marymount University, and the convention hotel was the Sheraton Gateway at LAX. I didn't know what to expect at this convention. I did not promote it widely throughout our BSU, but I did share it with some of the emerging leaders. I found out that certain positions on the youth advisory board were unfilled, which meant that those interested could run and possibly win a position on the state board. Still uncertain what all this meant, I knew that we had students who were involved enough and ambitious enough to welcome this opportunity. Knowing that this convention would be a weekend long event, and the money that it would cost to attend, approximately $215 per student, only a few decided to go. As the weekend approached, I had settled on taking three students, all friends, who were running for our BSU President position for next year. Raven had decided to run for the position of Parliamentarian on the UBSUC board. Raven was an 11th grade student who had won the respect of all the BSU students by the way she spoke in meetings. She was extremely intelligent and very articulate. It reached a point that when she spoke, she completely commanded the room. She made such great points that everyone wanted to hear what she would say next. Raven was also very humble. She had a quiet demeanor. She carried herself around campus with a level of maturity that I don't often see. She was an excellent student and was also involved in the AMPA as a singer in the school choir. Another student who would be attending this convention was Simone, also an 11th grader. Simone was already a leader on our campus as a member of the ASB. She too was a great student and was in contention to become the Student Body President in her senior year. Simone was well-known and liked by everybody, and also respected by everyone. She was the junior class President, and as such, very confident in leadership roles and working with adults. Simone was mature beyond her years, the kind of student I knew would be successful in whatever she chose to do. Both Raven and Simone would be great representatives of our BSU at this convention. The third student I was glad to bring was Colette. She was good friends with both Raven and Simone. She was an 11th grader as well, and though she had not had a leadership role in our BSU, Colette was a very dedicated and reliable member. I watched her grow from being a shy student, not very talkative, into a very confident young lady during her time in our BSU. The three of them would share a room together for the weekend, and now the only thing I needed to do was find a female chaperone. This would be my first time taking BSU students to an overnight trip, and as to be expected, I developed a very good line of communication with all their parents, who were all kind and very supportive of this opportunity for their daughters. I am eternally grateful for Ms. Saafir, a colleague at Hamilton whom I had gotten to know during the school year who accepted my request to chaperone the students. Of course I would be there, but I could not be with the students overnight and do room checks and things of that nature. In fact, since I didn't live very far from the hotel I just stayed home overnight and drove back each morning. I would be there in minutes if I was needed throughout the night, but I had complete confidence in my colleague. Our new BSU t-shirts had arrived the day of the trip and now we were all set to go. I packed the girls in my car and drove to the hotel. When we arrived, the girls took their belongings into their room and we gathered in the ballroom, and at that moment, I knew this was where we needed to be. Throughout the room at each table there were BSU students from schools representing all parts of California, and as proud as I was to be there representing our BSU with my three students and Ms. Saafir, I was equally perplexed at the lack of students from the vast Los Angeles Unified School District, at a convention in Los Angeles. I told Ms. Washington that night that Hamilton is here to stay, but the seed was planted then to see if more LAUSD schools would or could participate in an event like this going forward. That opening night the attendees were treated to a performance by the Foshay High School band as well as motivational speeches, and a delicious meal, with a full day planned for tomorrow. As I walked around and took pictures, I was filled with pride to see all these students and they all seemed very willing to get to know students from the other schools. I could see that my students were excited and ready for a fun weekend. I arrived at the hotel early the next morning and met the girls for breakfast in the ballroom. Since meals were included in the cost of the convention the students were fed well every breakfast and dinner at the hotel. Lunch would be provided at LMU later in the day. All around the room I could hear the buzz of excitement about the night before and what was to come. Soon after breakfast, buses would come to pick the students up to transport them to LMU where they would attend various workshops that focused on a number of important issues in the black community. They would attend two workshops and then gather in a lecture hall to hear the speeches of those running for office. What was also very impressive about this Saturday portion of the convention was there was a dress code of business attire. Part of the registration information included the dress code for each day of the convention and so the students were prepared and they all indeed looked ready for business. We found out that the position of President on the youth advisory board was vacant and Simone decided to represent the Southern region, and go for it. There are seven state youth advisory board positions. They are President, 1st Vice President, 2nd Vice President, Secretary, Treasurer, Parliamentarian, and Sergeant at Arms. What I discovered was that each state position consists of the winners of those same positions at the regional level. Each region holds a Regional Conference in the fall where each of those seven positions are chosen at the regional level. During the State Convention in the spring, those regional winners all compete for those same respective positions at the state level. This year, the positions of President and Parliamentarian in the Southern region were vacant, and the UBSUC constitution allows for students from the floor to seek those positions at the state convention. Enter Raven and Simone. They were not present at the fall conference, but somehow those two positions were open by the time of the State Convention, and knowing my students like I do, I knew they would step up. At the delegate assembly, the candidates for each position say their speeches as they are called to do so. Once the speech portion is over, the students will have the opportunity to then go around and meet with all the convention attendees and campaign for themselves and this is usually done during lunch. After watching Raven and Simone give their speeches, I sat with Colette during this beautiful Saturday afternoon on LMU's campus where they provided lunch outdoors on a grass quad. I watched with pride as my two students went from table to table meeting and greeting with the other BSU students looking very comfortable in the campaign process. Though we were small in number, Hamilton was making a strong impression. When lunch ended, we went back to a classroom where the students were re-introduced to all the candidates and then time was given for each school to caucus and determine their choice. Each school gets ten votes per position to divide them however they choose for each candidate. For example, if there are three candidates for Secretary, the voting school's spokesperson may say, "Los Angeles High School casts its votes as follows, 6 votes for candidate X, 2 votes for candidate Y, and 2 votes for candidate Z." The voting school can cast all ten votes for one candidate if it so chooses. The Parliamentarian explained these instructions to the schools and off they went to cast their votes. The votes are all counted by BSU advisors present, and

I was one of the vote counters for this convention's delegate assembly. The votes were counted, but the results would not be announced until the end of the convention. This is the same process for the Regional Conferences in the fall. The last part of the daytime session at LMU was a tour of the campus led by students from their BSU. After the tour, the buses were there to take the students back to the hotel where they would have about a two-hour break, and then it was time for the Saturday evening portion of the convention. The evening portion consisted of a banquet which included a nice dinner and an awards ceremony. After the awards ceremony, there was the much-anticipated dance. The dress code for this portion called for semi-formal attire, and again all the students looked very nice, like you might see at a Homecoming Dance. During the banquet, there were students awarded with scholarships and there was also the BSU of the Year award given out. I wasn't too aware of the BSU of the Year award at that time, but I thought it was great to recognize the individual scholars as well as the BSU in this way. When the ceremony was over it was time to move the tables back and make way for the dance floor. As nice as the students all looked, this was the moment they had been waiting for. When the deejay started with the first song the students were on the floor, and it seemed that they didn't stop until the last song of the night. The adult advisors rotated from chaperoning in the ballroom to going out into the lobby to rest and talk with one another. That's a nice way of saying we were all exhausted and simply could not keep up with the youngsters. The dance ended at about midnight and we had ordered pizza so the students could retire to their room for the night, as they had certainly worked up an appetite. There was only the Sunday portion of the convention left. Over breakfast the students were treated to an inspirational message before hearing the results of the delegate assembly. "For the position of Parliamentarian," the announcer read, "congratulations to Raven Maxwell!" I was thrilled to know that we had a representative on the state board. Unfortunately, Simone was not elected President, but she would serve out her senior year as President of the Southern region. Hamilton was now in the house and there would be no turning back. The last part of the convention was an emotional Rites of Passage ceremony where all of the graduating seniors lined up around the perimeter of the ballroom and proceeded around the room to be greeted by all the adults who gave them words of encouragement and appreciation.

The Rites of Passage concluded a long weekend where there was very little down time. There was a scheduled break of two hours the entire weekend. The rest of the time, other than sleeping overnight, was accounted for in the itinerary. When it was finally over, the students were extremely tired as you might imagine, but they had such a good time. As I waited with the girls in the lobby for their parents to pick them up, I had already decided that next year I wanted to take more students. Next year the Northern region would be hosting which meant we would be traveling. Unsure of the exact dates and location, all I knew was that we had to raise money, but we would be there.

This particular year Hamilton had the great fortune of becoming part of the UCLA-LAUSD Collaborative. This was a group of high schools in our district who, in partnership with UCLA, were put together to provide services and exchange ideas with the goal of making African American students more competitively eligible to attend UCLA, or at least attend a university coming out of high school. Because of events like African American Family Day, I was able to see where other schools were with their BSU's, at least the schools in our area. In this collaborative, I now could see BSU's from other parts of the district such as the schools in the San Fernando Valley and South Bay. With all the information we were receiving from these gatherings, I thought my contribution to the group could be in the area of BSU development, and how a club like a BSU could actually improve students' academic performance. People are always shocked and amazed when they hear the number of students in our BSU, but numbers are really based on the demographics. At Hamilton, we have a relatively large Black student population, so naturally our potential to have a lot of students in BSU is greater than schools with a small population of Black students. I would point those interested in our BSU to the consistency of the large numbers more than anything. How and why is it that year after year so many students at Hamilton seek out, sign up, and get involved with the BSU. That would lead one to ask what we do, and how do the students feel upon joining and becoming active. Immediately you would hear words like "family", "safe space," and "sense of belonging." These are characteristics BSU's can have regardless of numbers. When you add love, respect, and an emphasis on academic achievement and/or improvement, and at last patience, then you will see BSU actually help improve students' academic performance, provided that assistance is available when necessary. Simply stated, a BSU can inspire students to work harder and give them the motivation they need to take ownership of their academic experience. I have witnessed this time and again over my years at Hamilton.

A meeting was held at the end of the year to highlight some of the graduating seniors from the schools in the collaborative and to encourage the high achieving juniors as they go into their senior year. This would make our fourth trip to UCLA this year, as we had recently had our tenth graders there for their Buddy Day trip. This time I was asked to bring two seniors and a junior to this recognition meeting/luncheon. I chose to bring Aretha, Simone, and one more of our top seniors who had been accepted into UCLA named Larry, our only UCLA admit that spring. I always wanted to bring students who would be attending the school to events like this, and I knew Simone would be applying next year as well. It is always so gratifying to see my BSU students representing our BSU off campus and this was no different as each shared their experience and their future plans.

It was now the end of my seventh year as advisor, and like always, what was left was to install the new officers for next year. All the other positions for 2017-18 year were filled and the time came to interview our four candidates for President. Allissa was added to the group as she expressed her interest in running for President to me earlier in the spring. Allissa was an extraordinary dancer with whom I grew close like so many other students. She had not had a leadership role, but we talked often about classes, teachers, her future plans, etc. As a result of these conversations, many students grow in their commitment and participation in BSU. I applaud Allissa for running, and she actually did a good job. However, in the end, this very close competition resulted in Raven being selected as BSU President. I named Simone as Vice President, and Colette for Secretary. The graduation that year was at West Los Angeles College, and once again it was so good to see all the BSU graduates cross the stage. I was so happy to see our 2014 President, Camille, come back to support Aretha. The two had grown close over the years and their relationship exemplified the family that our BSU had become. The next year I would be reaching out to all the past Presidents, and they would eventually start a group chat so they can connect, keep in touch, and welcome subsequent Presidents to the group. The events of the next year provided great news to share with everyone connected to our BSU.

8
Renewed Energy

A few weeks after the graduation of 2017 I celebrated a milestone of sorts. It was my 50th birthday and for me a time of deep reflection. I spent a lot of time that summer evaluating every aspect of my life, my goals, and particularly my relationships. I also spent a lot of time thinking about my mother, and my commitment to making her proud. The one thing that made both my parents prouder than anything was the role I played in the lives of children, especially my own. Yes, they were proud grandparents, but they often commented on how it felt to see me with my two children. That pride also extended to my basketball teams in the past and to my role with BSU, they loved to see me interact with young people. With these relationships in mind, I entered the 2017-18 school year with renewed energy and a focus on building our BSU brand on and off campus.

We were coming into the school year with yet another very strong Executive Board. Much like my first year, the leaders of our BSU were also the leaders of the school. Raven was not in ASB, but Simone, our VP, did become Student Body President. Other strong additions to our board included our Historian Ti'Ara, who was quick to point out the correct pronunciation of her name, tee-AR-uh, and not tee-ERR-uh. She was always handy with the camera and did a great job capturing BSU events just like Matthew the year before. The family aspect of our BSU was always at play, as I went to church as a teenager with TiAra's mother, and I knew Ti'Ara when she was just a baby. Mychael "Michael with a Y" Carter, was our Treasurer. Mychael was the third Carter that I have had in my BSU. He is the younger brother of Maya from the class of 2014 and Cymone from the class of 2017. The first time I saw Mychael was when I dropped Maya off at home from school, of course with the permission of her guardian. I literally thought I was looking at the late Kobe Bryant. It was amazing to me how a person could look so much like someone else who was totally unrelated. At the time Mychael was in the eighth grade. He didn't come to Hamilton right away, but eventually he did transfer from nearby Fairfax High School and our school, and particularly BSU would be the better for it. Kaylin was our Financial Secretary, also a very dedicated and hard-working student. Kaylin would later attend Cal State L.A. and play a key role in inviting our BSU to campus and establishing a strong relationship with the school. Our BSU Show production team included Bryce, an amazing spoken word artist who had all sorts of technical knowledge of how a show should be put together. There was Ammaya, a very talented dancer, who had a great personality and seemed to get along with everyone. Yvonne rounded out the trio. "Vonnie," as she was called, was talented and funny and would bring much humor to our show. Another future Yankee Bruin, Zeyna, was our Community Service Committee Chair. Zeyna was another ASB student who was well-known and liked by everyone, as was Atiyyah, our Social Activities Committee Chair. Aliah and Elisha were now in their third year as grade level representatives, this time as juniors. It was hard to believe that Aliah was already a junior. She too was an ASB student, and a member of our very good girl's basketball team. This was the same Aliah whose mother I happened to see in the hallway during early registration as Aliah was entering high school. The woman was pushing a toddler in a stroller and looked like she didn't quite know where her destination was. I stopped and asked if she needed help, and when she turned around I said, "Nicole," as in Nicole Legaux who I coached during one summer while she played basketball for St. Mary's High School. Here she was now enrolling her daughter in Hamilton High School. I had not even met Aliah at that time, but I knew she would be a class act because I knew Nicole, and Nicole's father Cliff. A great family would be represented by Aliah and for four years she was an absolute star. When I talk about the amazing students I've gotten to work with over the years Aliah always comes to mind. Myles was now in tenth grade and continued on as tenth grade representative, but Trevious could no longer fulfill his role. We had to find a replacement, but this one was easy. As soon as I heard Taylor speak at a meeting, as a ninth grader, I knew she would eventually become a leader of our BSU. There was an intellectual curiosity and a social consciousness that was evident when she spoke. However, there was no role in leadership at the time, but when a position opened up, especially the tenth-grade rep. position it was Taylor's if she wanted it. I met my first ninth grade rep during early registration just like the year before when I met Myles. In much the same way that I saw Nicole in the hallway, I saw a mother and her daughter outside in our quad area who I thought might need some help, so I approached them, which was my role in assisting with early registration. I noticed the mother was a member of the Greek community as she was proudly wearing her Sigma Gamma Rho t-shirt. I introduced myself and asked if they needed help, and she said, "This is my daughter Kaelynn, and I'm Marquessa. Where is the textbook room?" I could have just pointed them in the direction, but I wanted to walk and talk with them, as I loved interacting with the new ninth graders as they are coming in. I quickly realized that Kaelynn was no ordinary ninth grade student. She was mature beyond her years, very intelligent, articulate, and ambitious. She sounded like she had her whole high school experience planned out. Well of course I began to talk to them about our BSU and made sure she included that as part of her experience by putting her on the Executive Board. The mom was also excited to know that we were active with the Divine Nine organizations and offered her assistance and support when needed. Advisors must realize that there are people who stand ready, and are willing to help you with your BSU efforts if you can build those relationships. It often just takes one conversation.

As usual the early weeks were for the Executive Board to meet and get to know one another while planning out the year. The committee chairs decide which days of the week they want to meet. The entire board looks at the calendar to see when we can organize certain events. Back-to-School Night, Club Rush, our first meeting, and then the mixer are always the events to get the year started on the BSU calendar. The biggest of these, Club Rush, yet again yielded a very large turnout of students and it really gets the student body excited about what BSU might have going on in the school year. We rolled into our first meeting of the year with a membership of 494 students signed up for BSU. Now again, 494 students don't attend every meeting each week. However, over the course of the year, the vast majority of those students will have attended at least one meeting, participated in at least one BSU event, and all will have sat down with me or the leaders individually or in small groups to talk about a BSU opportunity, or just what being in BSU means. Those first four events take us into October when most schools have their Homecoming events. At Hamilton that includes a Spirit Week during the week of the game, the tailgate on the day of the game, the game itself including the halftime festivities, and then the dance the next day. This school-wide celebration is organized by our ASB. The BSU involvement in the week would be to sell food during tailgate and during the game. Hamilton High School is one of the few schools that does not have lights on the football field, so our games are all day games. For Homecoming, however, lights are brought in which allows the students to have a true Friday night experience. In addition to having the night game, students are treated to a fireworks show at halftime. It is truly an incredible experience, especially because it only happens once a year. On this fun-filled Friday night there I was with Raven and other students at the BSU table selling barbecue link dinners for our BSU. By halftime we were completely sold out. It's always a sacrifice for those working the table because I know the students want to enjoy the game in the stands with their friends. This is a testament to those who stayed to work the table.

When the job was done, they still got to enjoy the game. It is never difficult to find someone in BSU to serve. My experience has been that when I ask someone outside of the board to serve in some way, they consider it an honor to be asked. I do this quite often as it helps me build relationships with the members that I do not interact with on a regular basis. After Homecoming Week, the BSU had three important activities scheduled before the Thanksgiving Holiday.

We had our annual senior Buddy Day trip to UCLA, and this time I took about 25 seniors, but what a wonderful experience it was. We were greeted by the UCLA buddies which included five former Hamilton BSU students. This trip has truly become almost like a reunion, and I am sure the alumni buddies are as proud as I am when we arrive on campus. I usually send out a group text to former BSU students who are current Yankee Bruins letting them know we are on campus and this time I was able to reach Dou'jae who came and had lunch with me. When she shared with me her course load and the fact that she was working, I felt honored that she would take time out for me. It's such a proud moment for me to see how well these students are doing in college and to know I had something to do with their preparation and development.

It was time now for the district-sponsored Young Men of Color Leadership Conference. It would be my second consecutive year attending. My plan was to continue to take ninth graders to this conference, and bring the previous ninth graders. This would be a good platform for leadership training and development for ninth and tenth graders. This year, however, it was a little different because I would be bringing my own son this time. Isaiah was attending Serra High School, a private Catholic school at the time as a ninth grader. There was a possibility his mother and I might transfer him to Hamilton, but we wanted to wait until after his first semester was finished. With about a month to go until that time, and since this trip was on a Saturday, I wanted him to experience this conference with Hamilton students. As you might imagine...he hated it. He didn't know any of the young men going. He was giving up a Saturday. He didn't want to go and his dad was making him go. In addition to all that, he had to wear a tie... let that sink in for a minute. This time the conference was held at LA Trade Technical College. It was a great day to spend with my guys and get to know them a little better. Skyler was a young man that I got to know pretty well on this trip. He was one of the ninth graders, and on this day, I learned that he was a musician, a bass player at that. I had been trying to teach myself to play bass for a while and here I was hanging with a freshman who was an established bass player who happened to know my favorite bass player, Marcus Miller. I would have been thoroughly impressed just to know that, but then I found out that Skyler was also a boxer, and to top that off, he was being picked up by his dad later because he had a basketball game. I would get to know Skyler's family quite well over his four years of high school. His twin sister Sierra would become a leader of our BSU, and his mother Lisa, a key parent and organizer of our BSU parent group. Again, I stress family. This is a perfect example of how a relationship with one student that started with a simple conversation turned into another bond that strengthened our BSU family. Speaking of family, Isaiah was in fact transferred into Hamilton after the first semester. I would again have the privilege and opportunity to see my child grow up through the high school years with me every day, what a blessing!

This year a very important addition was added to our November calendar. The UBSUC

Southern Region Conference was held at Cal State Northridge, and after attending the state convention last Spring, I was looking forward to this conference. I now had a general idea of how the conference would work and this time I took about 10 students. As officers on the board, Raven and Simone were on the program. Everyone else would be attending for the first time and I encouraged each one to run for a position on the board. Since seniors were not allowed to run for office in the fall, I brought all tenth and eleventh graders. At first no one wanted to run for a position, but on the bus ride to CSUN as we discussed the opportunity, they began to change their minds. They huddled up and discussed who would run for what so that they would not compete with each other. By the time we arrived, everyone had decided to run for a position. Our candidate for first Vice President would be Andre, a natural born leader, creative and spontaneous, who knew how to bring people together and was as cool as can be under pressure. He was also a very good athlete. I met Andre during his freshman year when I was Athletic Director. By the time he was a sophomore I had told him I wanted him to get more involved in BSU. His older sister Taryn was already active in BSU, and during this his junior year I could see him becoming more committed. Deborah, also a junior, decided to run for second Vice President. "Debbie Deb," as I call her was a self-proclaimed nerd. She was very intelligent, articulate, and another student who I had my eye on the moment I heard her speak at a meeting. She was a quiet, kind of shy student, but eventually would emerge as one of our leaders. From our BSU Executive Board running for positions would be Aliah, who was running for Secretary, Elisha for Parliamentarian, and Taylor for Sergeant at Arms. Lastly, Savannah would be running for the position of Treasurer. What was exciting about this group is what I alluded to before. Only three of the six were on our Executive Board. The other three, Andre, Deborah, and Savannah were great examples of non-board members who feel honored when asked to represent BSU. All three of them would eventually become Executive Board members. To begin the conference each school sat at their own table. I was again surprised to see so few LAUSD schools in attendance. This time the only other LAUSD school was Palisades. When the students were moved to other tables so they can share with students from other schools, it was a great chance for me to see how they interacted with other peers. I was delighted and very proud to see

205

that when the time came to share out, a Hamilton student was the spokesperson at each table. That picture validated for me our emphasis on leadership development. I believe in giving our BSU students many opportunities to lead in meetings, large and small. They are encouraged to develop opinions on what matters to them because they often have great insight and perspectives to contribute. I want them to know that what they feel matters. It's not that they are better than anyone else. It's knowing they are special and uniquely made and the community and the world needs to hear what they have to say. Thus, when put in a position to lead, our BSU students move toward and not away from those opportunities. I watched Taylor, a sophomore, lead her table conversation as if she was a senior. I was extremely impressed, but not surprised.

When the time came for the candidates to give their speeches for their respective positions it seemed that the early nerves had faded away and they all went up to the podium with confidence. There were other really good candidates as well. We didn't have a candidate for President, but after all the schools got a chance to hear from the candidates and then cast their votes, we ended up with four students on the Southern Region UBSUC

Youth Advisory Board. Andre, Deborah, Savannah, and Elisha were all elected for their positions. That meant that out of the seven positions on the board, four would go to Hamilton students. It was also very gratifying to see our President, and board Parliamentarian, Raven, swear the new board in. These four students would help create and plan all Southern Region activities for the next year and have a chance to compete in the Spring at Sacramento State University, the host of our Spring Convention. Though Aliah and Taylor didn't win their respective races, they remained very important parts of our BSU, and as important as it is to encourage students to put themselves out there and take the challenge and the risk of running for office, it is equally important to have the structure that supports them if they don't win. Our students, again because of the relationships, do a great job of supporting one another in this way.

The most exciting time of the year for our BSU is Black History Month. It is also the best time to see the BSU's impact on the school. One of the favorite activities of the month is Greek Week, and if that was debatable before, it wouldn't be after this year. We started off the week with our visit from the Alphas and AKA's. The two organizations were greeted in our meeting room which happened to be a dance studio, which set the stage for the inevitable. The students knew that this year for the first time, our finale to Greek Week would be a Yard Show on the quad this Friday. While the two organizations gave their presentations, and began to take questions from the students someone asked if they could do a step. The three Alpha brothers came ready for that request. They lined up in formation and the leader began to call out, "We are the brothers of the...." I looked out at the students and they were completely mesmerized as the Alphas went into their brief step routine. When they were finished students clapped and shouted with enthusiasm. I told them this was only a preview of what was to come on Friday, and to make sure they got out to the quad early so they could stand up front. For the rest of the day, I could hear the students talking about what happened at lunch and how they could not wait until Friday. On the next day, the second day of Greek Week we were honored to welcome a representative of Sigma Gamma Rho Sorority, Inc., and it happened to be Marquessa, who I met during registration, and she presented with her daughter Kaelynn, who was an active member of the mentor program of

SGRho called the Rhoers. Did I mention there was a family atmosphere to our BSU that was becoming more and more evident and prevalent? Here was a mother and daughter, now one of our leaders, presenting at Greek Week, a day after our Vice President Simone's mother represented Alpha Kappa Alpha Sorority, Inc. I started to feel that family dynamic in the 2016 class, but now one could not help but feel it. It is important to share here that this family dynamic didn't just happen. Family is a core value of mine that I hold dear in my heart. Whenever I have been with a group of students for any length of time, I have been seen as a father figure by many of them. I have had such nicknames as "Uncle T" at Hamilton, and "Pops" by other students. As a coach, my players have commented that I have been like a father to them. This is not a role that I have ever sought, but always seems to find me. I have learned to embrace the role and take it seriously that young people see me this way. Quite naturally as BSU advisor this role followed. It did not begin this way, however, because it started out as a club just like any other. As the numbers grew, so did the organizational structure and it became more of an organization, but by 2016, and certainly by now it was more like a family. I always felt if I was there long enough it would take on a family feel, and we were certainly on our way. For other advisors, it may or may not be part of the mission to create a family bond within your BSU, but if it is, you will have to embrace the role as a mother/father figure to your students, not just teacher or mentor, and you will have to incorporate and include family members of your students when possible. It is also important to encourage your BSU students to see one another as brothers and sisters and to value each other as such. All those things have led to something really special on the campus of Hamilton High School, and I was glad to be a part of it.

The third day of Greek Week brought a very special guest and representative of Kappa Alpha Psi, Fraternity, Inc. One of our school police officers, Officer Jennings was a member, and he introduced me to Mr. Danny Tabor, former mayor of Inglewood, California. Mayor Tabor agreed to visit our campus and represent his fraternity on that Wednesday. He gave a very inspirational message to our students not only about his organization and his career, but also the importance of serving. As one of our guiding principles is service, I found Mr. Tabor's message timely and I was very appreciative. One of the things I hope to accomplish with Greek Week is to show the students the respect that members of these organizations have for one another, and that though they often compete, they are not enemies; that there is a great deal of support from one organization to another. Day four and the last day of the indoor presentations brought out the brothers of Omega Psi Phi Fraternity, Inc. and the sisters of Delta Sigma Theta Sorority, Inc. The Ques (Omega men), were represented by two men who were already working at Hamilton, and needless to say they couldn't wait for their turn. They knew what had been happening all week, and about the Yard Show on Friday, so when they got their chance to speak to the students, they brought great energy. Mr. Tolson, a former BSU student from 2012 had now joined our staff and was working in the AMPA program while finishing his teaching credential, was one of our speakers. He was joined by Mr. Jacqwel Brown, known as Mr. Q, a site coordinator with the Communities in Schools program that was on our campus. This program brought a lot of resources and individual tutoring and mentorship to our school, and was a great addition to our campus community. The Deltas were represented by our very own Ms. Cooley, and Ms. Dana Henry, who had been so instrumental in helping develop African American Family Day.

Ms. Henry no longer worked at the school, but she was as much a part of the BSU family as anyone. This was a fun day because the guests were not really guests. They were our very own and they engaged the students while they praised their respective organizations behind a table filled with paraphernalia that included jackets, hats, books, lanterns, shields, etc. It was a great way to finish off that portion of the week, and from that point on the excitement and anticipation grew as tomorrow would be our first ever BSU Yard Show.

That Friday the day could not have been more beautiful. It was sunny and warm and not a cloud in the sky. I had coordinated with alumni De'Ante King, Jolen Sanders, and Chantel Wiggins, Alpha Phi Alpha, Kappa Alpha Psi, and Zeta Phi Beta, respectively to bring members of their organizations to perform for us on that day. As lunch grew nearer my first guest arrived and it was Marquessa in her gold SGRho t-shirt. Then the Alphas showed up, four in number, and I met with them on the quad. Then Chantel showed up with her one of her sorors. She shared that it would be just the two of them on stage, but it didn't matter because I knew Chantel and the energy she would bring even if she was alone. Then from a distance I see the Kappas coming through the building to the quad. Everyone was on time. The speakers were set up. We started to play some music at a low volume because classes were still in session. Each organization was polishing up their routines and with a few minutes before the bell was to ring, I decided to turn up the music as I saw some of the students were coming out of class early. The excitement was palpable. When the bell rang, you could see the students running out to the quad. I stood there in all black with my Alpha jacket on and black jeans, music pumping loud, microphone in hand encouraging everyone to make it to the stage. When the quad looked like a sea of people, I welcomed everyone to the first annual Hamilton BSU Yard Show, and introduce our MC, the one and only Mr. Q, who took the mic and got everyone excited and loud before shouting, "PLEASE WELCOME THE LADIES OF ZETA PHI BETA SORORITY INCORPORATED!" Chantel took the mic and began to give a brief introduction of her sorority and her soror, who joined her on stage, before she goes into, "ONE... NINE... ONE, NINE, TWO, OH!" They go into their step routine and the crowd goes crazy. The seniors in the crowd remember Chantel when she was a senior during their freshman year. They all shouted and cheered as the two Zetas went from their step routine to a stroll to Ric Flair Drip, and then everybody went crazy. They finished to a loud cheer and then Q takes the mic and introduces the ladies of Sigma Gamma Rho Sorority, Inc. The surprise to everyone here was that Marquessa introduces the sorority, gives a brief history, and then calls Kaelynn to the stage. The music plays and they do a mother-daughter stroll. It was absolutely amazing. Interestingly enough, the two of them looked like college students on stage. Kaelynn was a pretty popular ninth grader, but I think she surprised everyone that day the way she strolled with her mom, and how comfortable she looked performing in front of this large crowd. That was a really good addition to the Yard Show. Now it was time for the Alphas. After Q brings them on stage, Ebreon takes the mic and gives a brief introduction of the fraternity including when and where we were founded, along with the recognition of those founders which we call our Seven Jewels. Ebreon was an Alpha who worked at the school representing the Early Academic Outreach Program at UCLA. He decided to join the brothers on stage. He finishes up with, "With that being said, enjoy the show." The Alphas go in their step and it was as though the crowd was studying every move. I heard someone say, "Oh they're really stepping." The routine was a lesson in precision as every clap, hiss, leg raise, head and arm movement were in perfect synchronization until the very end. There was a thunderous applause when they finished, but it wasn't over. The music began to play as they lined up to do their stroll, and then came more screaming and yelling from the crowd when after the second time around the stage they finished with their, "A..PHI...WHO YA WIT? ICE!!" More screaming. If that wasn't enough, the Kappas were introduced next. There were about five on stage and they begin to give their brief introduction before "Wipe me down" starts to boom through the speakers. The girls screamed even louder when the guys went into their shoulder shimmy move as they kneeled down. The crowd was completely into it, and then almost as if planned, Jolen arrived late and made his way through the crowd and joined his brothers on stage seemingly coming out of nowhere. It was too much. I was completely enjoying the excitement of our students, who certainly were having a great time, and now it was time for the last organization, the Omegas. Mr. Q enthusiastically introduced his organization and then Mr. Tolson took it from there. He gave a brief history of his organization and explained that the Omegas don't step. They

215

hop. And with that "Atomic Dog" begins to play and Mr. Tolson goes into his hop routine by himself. Then Mr. Q joins him and the two close out the Yard Show to a super loud applause. An applause that included many faculty members who had made it to the quad. It was an amazing thirty minutes. Before the bell rang we all got to take many pictures on stage. We took group photos with everyone. I got a chance to take a picture with all my alumni and I was filled with pride, and gratitude that they would come back and make this day so special. After lunch ended, we had an opportunity to visit our African American Literature class taught by Ms. Battle. The Kappas, Zetas, Sigma Gamma Rho, and myself visited and gave a united presentation of what our organizations have meant to the black community and the country as a whole. It was a great way to end an exciting and very successful day. This Yard Show set the bar high for all the others to come in the following years.

Another annual tradition we have in our BSU is the BSU Honor Roll. This is a new one however. When I moved out of the classroom into my office, I saw that there was a bulletin board in the hallway outside of the office, and no one had claimed to use it. I asked if it was ok for me to make that our BSU board to which I was granted permission. I keep the board updated with any BSU announcements as well as college posters that I have collected over the years. During the first semester, at the midterm, 10-week grading period, I post all the BSU students who have a 3.0 grade point average or above for each grade level. I divide them as follows: 3.0-3.49, 3.5-3.99, and 4.0 and above. I literally go through each student on the BSU roster and calculate the grade point average. I do this again at the end of the first semester so that when the students return from Christmas vacation, they can see the updated fall semester honor roll. Seeing this BSU Honor Roll has given the students a great deal of pride as they walk through the hall. I see many students stop and stare trying to find their name, and honestly most of the names of the BSU students are on the wall, but not all of them. It serves as motivation for those who are not there, and for those who are, they are always challenged to move up higher if they can. During the second semester, there is a lot posted about things like the BSU Show, or the Black College Expo, or even other flyers related to Black History Month, and it typically stays that way until May. After May 1, which is College Commitment Day, I begin to post pictures of the seniors who have made their commitment to a college. I will print their senior picture, which is the one in the formal attire, and then I have the logo of the school they chose placed in one of the corners of the picture. I got a lot of help with this from BSU parent Starr Thompson, whose son Aerick graduated the year before. The board itself holds about 26 8"X10" pictures, and when it fills up, I use the space on the wall around the board. Needless to say, this board gets a lot of attention from the those who walk the hallway. Unfortunately, some of the attention is not positive. Shortly after the new semester began a student, who might be described as an aspiring journalist, began taking a camera around school and interviewing students and even some teachers about whether or not there should be a BSU Honor Roll. I later found out that this topic was getting a lot of attention on social media as well. The student seemed to suggest that there should not be separate honor rolls, and that other clubs were not doing this. The student even asked to interview me. I arranged to meet with the student on three separate occasions, and on all three, the student didn't show up. I explained that there would not be another chance, as a major part of getting the interview, or job, or whatever it might be, is showing up. The BSU students were incensed as they felt like this was an attack on the brand that BSU has established over the years. They felt that any club could have done the same thing to highlight and publicize the academic excellence of its members. The fact that BSU was doing just that on the BSU board was not creating a separate list, but extracting from the already existing honor roll the students that were in BSU, the same way one would do to highlight any subgroup on the list. There was a major response from the alumni, which I did not expect. They came to the defense of BSU over the social media platforms and it was beautiful to see. Students from two and three years ago, before there was a BSU Honor Roll commented on our emphasis on academic excellence and that we always celebrated academic accomplishments. The students invited the journalist to a BSU meeting, and to his credit, he came and faced the large group who showed up to the meeting. He seemed to finally understand the reason for the honor roll, but he clearly did not understand the depth of the BSU brand on campus. We were doing things that no other club was doing and we had the support of the administration and the school community. We supported all the work the other clubs were doing as well. This seemed out of the norm for him. The truth is that it was out of the norm, for any club, even other BSU's. I knew this student, and I actually liked him. For him it was an education on the power of our BSU.

I was once again excited to take the students on our annual Pan African Film Festival trip. This time I would be taking my son for the first time. Like his sister he had heard all about the BSU activities over the years and it was now his turn to experience them for himself. The movie of choice was *Triumph: The Untold Story of Perry Wallace*. Perry Wallace was the first African American to receive a basketball scholarship and play in the Southeastern Conference of the NCAA when he attended Vanderbilt University in 1966. It was important for me when choosing a film to view at the festival to choose one involving students in some way, preferably high school or college students. This particular story was one I had not been aware of, which was surprising to me because I like biographical stories, especially sports stories. I personally found Wallace's story fascinating as one of my favorite sports stories is the college basketball championship won by Texas Western University and their all-black starting five over the all-white University of Kentucky basketball team, which took place the year before Wallace was to integrate the SEC. The students see college sports now and are amazed at how it used to be. Isaiah was one of only two ninth graders to attend this trip. I usually make it a point to include students of all grade levels, but admittedly there are usually far more juniors and seniors. Isaiah usually spends the nutrition and lunch breaks in my office. He comes across as shy initially, but he has always preferred not to be around lots of people. He has never felt the need to socialize very much at school, though he does talk during class, which is where he would usually meet any new friends. This trip was the first time he was able to spend lots of time around the older BSU students. They all knew of him and embraced him. I appreciated how they interacted with him, especially students like Mychael, Andre, and Justin who was very comfortable striking up a conversation with anyone. Justin Scott was in his second year at Hamilton. He moved from Baltimore and enrolled at Hamilton in his sophomore year. I was just getting to know him and I was extremely impressed with this young man. I would often see him with Andre and another young man, Dominic, whom I also met when I was Athletic Director during their freshman year. Now they were juniors, except for Mychael, and they would become very influential leaders on our campus. I wanted Isaiah to get to know these young men as I thought they were positive examples for any young freshman. These were the kinds of moments I really enjoyed with him as he was finding his way through high school. It was like that with all the students really. It was that time spent element of relationship building. It was the quality and quantity of time that we spend together that has made this BSU what it is.

When it was time for the BSU show at the end of the month the team had settled and been rehearsing for what could be a controversial show. The show was called "Dear Hamilton." This would be a show in which the students wanted to expose and address what they felt were many micro-aggressions they see and experience on campus. This was a group this year who had heightened sensitivities about words that were spoken to them and certain interactions with peers and adults on campus. These topics were the subjects of many BSU meetings. They wanted to show the audience how they felt about certain things that they hear on campus. There is no doubt that the honor roll controversy played a part in some of the direction of the show. They had spent the year, at least to that point, feeling like they had to justify or explain either themselves, black culture in some way, or even more specifically our BSU. Sometimes it was not racial insensitivities, but gender insensitivities that caused discomfort. It was time to respond in the students' eyes and that's what they did in a very good BSU show. As some shows may feature more acting, singing, or dance, this one was heavy on spoken word. As we were rehearsing some of the pieces in the auditorium the band, our house band, happened to be there. When Mychael was rehearsing on the microphone, I asked the saxophonist, Ronnie, to play something softly to Mychael's cadence. Suddenly the piece took on a new flavor and we decided to include music in a few of the pieces. This is just how it worked when we prepared for a show. In the past, we used our jazz band sometimes to play entrance and exit music as the classes were coming and going between shows. Before that, I played music on our sound system during that time. This year was the first year that the band was actually a part of the show and it was a nice touch. From then on, we would appoint one of the musicians, who was also in BSU, to put the musicians together and form our "house band" for the show. These were students who were always creating even during breaks at school. I would walk by and hear them working on raps or poems, or they might be in our new sound lab making beats. When it was time to put it all together on stage in the show, it came very naturally.

The reason why an otherwise controversial show turned out to be so successful was that the students who wrote the script and acted out the parts were truly respected on campus and they had these types of conversations with their peers, both black and white. This is why leadership is so important. You want students who carry themselves like leaders to run your BSU. They are in the room when those tough conversations are held and they know how to communicate without losing their audience. They have informed opinions and their intellect is respected. I have just described leaders like Raven, Simone, Zeyna, Atiyyah, and so many others. After a long month filled with excitement, I took a couple days off. It was almost time for the UBSUC State Convention in Sacramento. Before the convention however, there was another important event planned, not just at Hamilton, but across the country.

It had been about a month since the deadly school shooting at Stoneman Douglas High School in Florida, which captured national attention and gave every high school student, and employee cause to pause in fear. In my new position as

Restorative Justice Teacher/Advisor I held many community building circles with classes in the immediate aftermath to address the situation and to allow students to express how they felt about the shooting, and what we can do at Hamilton to help our students feel safe. There had been a national walk out and rally scheduled for the following month and sure enough our school leaders and BSU leaders would be right there out front when the day came. The "March For Our Lives" rally drew a lot of attention from the media as it was the students' way of letting the government know that there needs to be gun laws in place that protect students from these horrific events. They also wanted to encourage fellow classmates to look out for one another, especially those with mental health issues, and for those students to seek help if needed. There on the steps of the auditorium speaking through the bull horn was Simone and other school leaders, and a passionate message from a young man with a bright orange shirt, who knew how to fire up the crowd. His name was Justin Scott.

This would be our second trip to the State Convention, but our first true road trip. We had agreed to travel up north with Venice High School and Hollywood High School's BSU. I had worked with the advisors of both schools during our time hosting African American Family Day. Hollywood's advisor had left Venice to take a position at Hollywood and was now their advisor. We all got along really well and shared a mutual respect. Hamilton and Venice are rival schools, but when it came to BSU it was all respect. I took nine students on this trip, six girls and three boys. Andre and Dominic were both athletes as were some of the boys with the Venice group, so they knew each other from the games in which they competed. When we were all on the bus and finally on the road it was great to see how the students got along and were excited to see and get to know one another. As officers from the previous year, Raven and Simone had their room payed for as is the procedure for all state officers. My two eleventh grade reps, Aliah and Elisha were on the trip as well as Deborah and Savannah. They all shared a room. Elisha, Deborah, and Savannah would all be running for state office during the convention. Andre would be running as well. Justin shared the room with Andre and Dominic, and that accounted for our nine students. This is the time of year when students normally make their interest known for a position on our Executive Board. We had stopped about halfway to Sacramento to stretch and get a bite to eat, and I sat near Raven and Simone, who were having a conversation with Justin. What I was witnessing at that very moment was three of our school's most outstanding leaders, and I wondered if they were talking about Justin running for President of our BSU for the following year. Days before the trip I had communicated with my former BSU student Maurice, who was attending Sacramento State. We arranged for him to meet the group as we arrived at the hotel. Sure enough, as the bus pulled into the parking lot, there he was. We unloaded our luggage from the bus compartment and right there in the parking lot I introduced him to the group. They were all ninth and tenth graders when Maurice was a senior. Maurice was very active in BSU, particularly in the shows, but he was always such a great representative of what BSU was on campus. He was never involved in any negativity. He went to his classes, got along well with all his teachers. He talked to the students about what BSU meant to him during his time at Hamilton, a time before we were involved with the UBSUC. He thought it was great to have this opportunity to go to conventions, and told them to enjoy every moment of it and to represent. He shared with them how things were going for him as a Theater major at Sacramento State, expressed his pride in all of them, and wished them well. We finally went inside to check in, get room keys, and settle in. I hear a knock at my door and it was Simone with great news. She had just found out she got accepted into UCLA. I was so excited for her. She had worked so hard for this, and I knew that was where she wanted to go. All this before we even made it to the ballroom for the start of the convention. This was a great way to start the weekend. We got to the ballroom for dinner to get us started and then there was a welcome and roll call. Each school present was called upon to do their school chant. Well, with Andre and Domo (Dominic's nickname), present I knew they would have something ready for when Hamilton was called. "Domo, gimme dat beat!" Domo starts to pound his fist on the table and then they all caught the cadence and joined in. Andre begins his call and response to the other students and they all got hyped up. I just smiled and laughed, and thought to myself, "The Yanks are here now." The highlight of the evening was an inspirational spoken word performance by "Coon the Poet." He was an outstanding artist who before long had the whole audience spellbound. I looked at my students and at least the young men were hanging on his every word. Later they gave the students a chance to take the mic and show their skills. Andre got his turn and did a rap that everyone seemed to really like. It was the same one he did in the BSU show and they were really feeling it. Then he looked at me as I was recording him and gave me some recognition as someone they all looked up to like a father. It was a proud moment for me, but it was also exciting to see the students having so much fun. The next day would be a very busy day. We got up and had breakfast and then boarded the bus to Sacramento State. The students were dispersed into various workshops until about noon when lunch was to be provided in the cafeteria. After lunch it was time for the delegate assembly in one of the school's multi-purpose rooms. There were probably about 250 students attending the convention. Each student who got up to speak had to look out at this huge audience of their peers. The candidates for each position gave their speeches and I remember how poised and confident each of my students were. I felt that each one of them did well enough to win their respective races. Of course the results would not be announced until the next day at the hotel. When the candidates were finished speaking and each school had a chance to caucus and then cast their votes, we were given a tour of the university and then finally taken back to the hotel. The students had about a two-hour break until the evening festivities were to begin. I spent that time with my cousin Teonie who lives in Sacramento and came to visit me at the hotel. Some students hung out at the pool while others went to their room and rested before changing into their banquet outfits. At the banquet, the scholarships were given out and then it was time to give the award for BSU of the year. When the announcer gave the criteria for the award and then began to read off the accomplishments of the winning BSU, I realized that she was reading off all the things that we were able to do during the year and I knew then that we had won. When she said, "the BSU of the Year award goes to Hamilton High School," I was filled with joy and so proud of the students at the convention and all those back at home. It was only our second year in the UBSUC, but this award validated for me all of the work that had been put into developing this club and leading this family. It was a tribute to all the past Presidents and leaders over the years. We simply had done throughout the year as we always had done. The candidates for BSU of the year have to apply for the award and self-report all of the school's activities including any pictures or videos that support those activities. We never know how many schools nominate themselves for the award, it's hard to say who the competition is. All the schools present at the convention have BSU's who are very active and also have dedicated advisors. There is an advisor's meeting that usually takes place on the first night of the convention when the students have their time of opening night entertainment. After the awards were given out and dinner was finished, it was time for the dance. Just like the year before in Los Angeles, the students had their time to party on the dance floor and the adults tried our best to enjoy the evening with them. We danced when we could and we also had time to socialize with one another in shifts. We played cards and dominoes and just had a good time catching up. We alternated going into the ballroom to make sure the students were being supervised appropriately, but there were no problems. They all had a great time. By the time the dance ended we had ordered pizza for the students, which is our usual routine to close out the evening as we sent them to their rooms for the night. The next morning, they all sluggishly came down to the ballroom for breakfast and the last few hours of the convention. They were treated to a performance by a praise dance team and then received another inspirational message, and then it was time to announce the results of the elections. For the position of Parliamentarian, it was announced that Elisha Gutierrez was the winner. For Treasurer, the winner was announced as Savannah Moten. For 2nd Vice President, Deborah Gallego, and for 1st Vice President, Andre Hustace. All four Hamilton students won their positions on the state board. They would lead the state board from spring until next spring when they pass the torch to the new winners at the convention. Since they also won in the fall, they would serve out their term as Southern Regional board members until the fall conference in November. This was a very successful convention for our BSU and a fun convention for our students to attend. Everyone was extremely tired on the way home and the road trip gave everyone a chance to catch up on some sleep. I, however, took the time to text all of our past Presidents, all seven of them together, and thank them and give them the news that our BSU has been awarded California's BSU of the Year. They were all extremely proud of the news. They congratulated me and wanted me to pass on their words to the students. It was my first time texting all the Past presidents together, but it was not surprising to read from Alexander that they would keep this group chat and communicate together welcoming in each new President into the group. Raven, as the current President would be the latest one added. We finally made it home and by now there were a few more events on our BSU calendar before the year was over. We had our spring Buddy Day trip with the sophomores and we still had to install officers for the next year.

When the sophomores had their trip to UCLA we took a solid group of tenth graders. They were all top students and I knew they would get a lot out of the trip. I also took Kaelynn even though she was only in the ninth grade. It was another successful trip and the Hamilton alumni were some of the main chaperones. This time we had Chantel, Jolen, and Camille, who would be graduating from UCLA in just a few weeks. Simone, Zeyna, and Abeni would later take their traditional picture with the Bruin bear as the newly accepted Yankee Bruins. The group that attended this trip would have the most interesting of senior years.

For the first time since I was in high school, I decided I would attend the senior prom. I could have gone to any of the proms in previous years, but for some reason I really wanted to enjoy this evening with this class. I think we had grown so close, and so many of the students had asked that I come that it just felt like I couldn't miss it. The

233

prom was held at Universal Studios and, of course I had to buy a nice new suit. I ended up wearing a three-piece black suit with a gold tie, representing my fraternity colors of course. I had a great time with my colleagues who were there to chaperone. Everyone looked so nice and there were times I just sat back and reflected on all the fun this year provided. The year before, in the 2017 class, I took a collection of pictures that were sent to me and made a prom edition to our website. I was at the champagne party for my cousins E'mon and D'mon who graduated that year and they looked spectacular that night. Kenya's prom was the year before that. I guess for the two years before this class I had seen my students going to the prom and heard my colleagues telling me how nice it was, it made me want to see for myself. I am so glad I went. It was great to see the students dressed up for the last time. Later they had a great time at their Senior Picnic and I drove a cart around and took lots of pictures on that day as well. Then there was Senior Awards Night when for the first time, I was asked to give out awards to BSU seniors. This was an annual event at the school, but now BSU was given a chance to award specifically black students. I was honored to give out awards to my amazing students, and I decided to give out five awards.

One for each one of our principles: an Outstanding Scholarship Award to the highest gpa, an Outstanding Leadership Award, and a Commitment to Service award. Then I decided to give two awards called the BSU Award of Excellence to two students who exemplified our principles for their entire four years of high school. The scholarship award was given to Jordan Bucknor. The leadership award was given to our President Raven, and the service award was given to Atiyyah. The awards of excellence were given to Simone and Zeyna. It was as though the last day of school was taking forever and all these events were just ways to slowly say goodbye until graduation day.

Meanwhile we were getting next year's Executive Board ready and during this time I got a chance to meet and work with Darnell Sapps, a new representative with the Communities in Schools program at our school site. Darnell was a young and passionate advocate for students and would be a great addition to our BSU family. He stood for everything we were about and made himself available for any assistance that I would need going forward with BSU. It was great to have him by my side going forward. The new board was complete and interviewing the presidential candidate in this case was just a formality. Justin had emerged as such a clear favorite to become our next President that he ran unopposed, not because everyone was afraid to run, but because everyone truly wanted him to be the President. He had earned that respect from the BSU leaders and from the school as a whole. He did have to go through the process anyway, and he did receive some tough follow up questions from Taylor, but in the end we all celebrated when he was announced as President because we knew what kind of year the class of 2019 would be.

I had a practice of purchasing Kente cloth graduation sashes for the seniors since 2014. At first, I would go downtown and purchase the sashes myself and then sell them to the students until they were gone. I would have as many as I could find in the stores downtown and therefore only maybe 20 students or so would get one. I found a company based in Ohio and I started purchasing the sashes from him. He would make as many as I needed, so I had the students pre-order their sashes this year. The problem was I placed the order so late that the sashes arrived actually on graduation day. I had to stay at the school and wait for the sashes to arrive via FedEx. I then had to drive them to the new site of our graduation, the

Greek Theater. When I arrived at the Greek, I had to find a few students to help me distribute the sashes to everyone who purchased one. It was a hot day and I had to walk back and forth looking for certain students until all the sashes were gone. I was finally able to put on my gown as I was in the graduation processional and would be sitting on the stage. The time had finally arrived and the graduation had begun. What a beautiful day it was. The students all wore green caps and gowns and the black Kente cloth sashes signaled which students were in BSU as one side of the sash read BSU and the other read Class of 2018. On my computer screen saver right now is a picture of one of my favorite students, Zeyna, who was Senior Class President speaking out to the crowd. It is a picture that symbolizes all that our BSU is to me. An outstanding student, the sweetest person imaginable, celebrating this great achievement and sharing words with the Hamilton family. The picture captures everything I celebrate about our students. I am inspired every time I look at it.

The 2018 school year was officially over. It included significant firsts for us including a Yard Show, a House Band in our BSU show, a BSU of the Year award, and BSU awards at Senior Awards Night. I had set out at the beginning of the year to build our BSU brand even more and these events were a testament to the growth of our BSU in just this year. We continue to do our annual events, but these additions gave us even more visibility and positive publicity on and off campus. With all that was happening, the most important thing was that the family was growing even stronger. On a personal note, to cap the year off, I was nominated and did win the prestigious NAACP Man of Valor Award for 2018 by the NAACP Youth Council. Our very own Dee Dee Sims, who was the President of the council, informed me that she was going to nominate me. I had never heard of the award and didn't realize that I had such an impact on this exceptional young student. I was truly honored to be nominated, and though I could not attend the ceremony because I was away at a conference, I did receive the recognition in the program with other men who were making significant contributions in the community. My dad was extremely proud, which filled me with joy. I only wished my mother was there to see. After this eventful year I was ready to celebrate another birthday in a week and then get ready for one of my greatest years as an educator.

Kenneth L. Turner

The Brand

9
When It All Comes Together

Going into the summer of 2018 I was finishing my 30th year as an educator. Much of that time I was both a teacher and a basketball coach. I have experienced lots of success on both fronts, as I tend to measure my personal success by the impact I had on the young peoples' lives after they are no longer with me. I know the impact that I have had because they tell me. They make sure I know that I played a certain role in their development as people and that is the reward that money cannot buy. That is all I want to do. Entering into my ninth year as BSU advisor I have either kept in touch with or have been visited by many alumni who share these sentiments with me, even up to the most recent nomination of the NAACP Man of Valor Award. As I write this paragraph, I am looking at the poetry book written by Dee Dee, who now goes by Nazeema. The signed book on the inside reads, "To Mr. Turner. Thank you so much for all that you have done and continue to do. I promise I'm going to make you proud." From Nazeema. With students like Nazeema, you will always have a successful BSU. If winning BSU of the Year was our "championship" of sorts, and it certainly had that feel, coming into this next year I felt like our "team" was even better, poised to repeat. It wasn't that we didn't feel the loss of the previous senior class, because you never forget your first one, and the leaders that made it happen; it was who was returning and their mindset coming into the year.

Justin was a straight A student who was committed to his education, very much involved in activism, and never concerned with what other students thought of him. He was extremely articulate, mature, and passionate about BSU. He was only our second male President in my nine years, and he was a true leader. He and Andre were a perfect team. Andre was 1st Vice President of the state board, and our Secretary, Deborah, was

2nd Vice President. Savannah was state board Treasurer, and she served the same position on our Executive Board. Our Financial Secretary was Aniya, one of our track and field athletes and a positive influence on campus. A key position for us is our Historian and that role was filled by Lela, who made it a point the previous spring to let me know that she wanted to get more involved in BSU, and then this role presented itself and she enthusiastically took it. Building our social media presence would be our Social Media Coordinator, Ericka. As is our tradition, I asked Bryce, who was one of our BSU Show production team members from the year before, who he would recommend to take that position for the following year. He suggested that I ask Treniece to lead the team. Treniece was another BSU student who was in our music academy. She was an extremely talented writer and spoken word artist. She had performed on stage many times and had the ability to not only write a good script, but put a very good team together. Treniece was excited to accept the position and immediately recommended an amazing dancer named Virginia to lead the choreography portion of the show. Keep in mind, we didn't even know what the show was going to be yet. This is simply how the team is assembled to take on the task. The third member was unanimously chosen by the two, and that was Aiyana. Like the other two, Aiyana had been very active in the music academy. She acted, sang, danced, and was a poet. Incredibly gifted in the arts, there was seemingly nothing Aiyana didn't do well. Additionally, Aiyana had a strong sense of pride in her blackness and in black culture and she communicated that very well in meetings. Our other three committees were led by experienced leaders on campus and BSU stars. The Community Service Committee Chair was Aliah, who had a been on the board since ninth grade, and the Social Activities Committee Chair was her best friend Elisha, who has served alongside Aliah as grade level reps the two previous years. The Fundraising Committee Chair, Ali, was also our Student Body President so there again was the connection to ASB, as several other ASB students were active in BSU. Rounding out the board were our grade level reps who would all eventually become major leaders in BSU and on campus. The eleventh-grade reps were again Taylor and Myles who served the previous year. The tenth-grade reps were two students who were added to the board late, but were really strong and perfect representatives of their class. Sierra was the twin sister of Skyler that I met on the Young

Men of Color Conference. She was an outstanding student and she was dedicated to BSU, a solid addition to the board. Sierra, along with Kaelynn and another BSU sophomore, Mateenah, had just participated in one of those opportunities that our students are exposed to thanks to the awesome outreach efforts at UCLA and our relationship with them. They attended a program for rising sophomores called Bruin Weekend, which is designed to identify and expose incoming tenth graders to an amazing experience and preview of what college can be like, both academically and socially. Events like these can become the spark that sets a student's mind on a particular path. I believe this did that for Sierra, who eventually got accepted into the VIPS program, and became another Yankee Bruin. Olivia Holley was the other rep, and when I met her, I knew she had to be on the board. I had been asked to visit a class where there was a substitute teacher who made some comments in class that the students took exception to. As the Restorative Justice teacher, it was my job to sit in and try to mediate a conversation between the teacher and students. This was a white teacher whose background had been at a small private school, quite a different demographic than the very diverse and large student body at Hamilton. This

245

particular class was an example of that diversity. The students were offended by the teacher's comment that they were "acting like animals." There had been more said, but that one was the one that was emphasized to me when this was brought to my attention. I was asked to visit the class along with the Director of the music academy, Ms. Freitag. While listening to both sides I noticed two new students who did most of the speaking on behalf of the class. I assumed they were new because I had not seen them before this year. These two young ladies were very articulate and very poised. They clearly held strong opinions that the class should not have been characterized that way, but it was the way they stated their position. They were very respectful and demonstrated an ability to listen with respect instead of just speaking and dominating the conversation. They were calm, which kept the rest of the class calm. They showed great leadership, and the ability to speak to power unlike I had seen in such young students. I called both students outside for a minute to speak with them privately, and I am sure they both thought they were in trouble. I looked at them and said, "I am so proud of both of you right now. I really appreciate the way you are representing your class. I need students like you to be leaders in BSU." One of those students was Olivia. They both thanked me for that affirmation and I was able to put Olivia on the board immediately because there was an opening. The other student was a ninth grader named Denim, like the jeans. I had been introduced to her earlier by Mychael, who had come back to Hamilton to work in the computer lab. Mychael walked me over to Denim one day and introduced us and told me to "keep your eye on this one." BSU had a huge effect on Mychael and he, like many other alumni, were very protective of the family. It had been a foregone conclusion in his mind that Denim would be in BSU and he wanted to make sure she represented in a positive way. That would prove to be the understatement of the year. I did not have a position on our board at the time for Denim because I filled the ninth-grade rep positions very early. The first one I met while she was in eighth grade. During the last year we had an opportunity to hear from Congresswoman Karen Bass, who is a Hamilton alumnus. When she came to speak at Hamilton, our nearby feeder school, Palms Middle School, sent a group of students to attend the event as well. When the event was over, I walked to where the excited middle schoolers were and I noticed this one student who stood out. She was clearly the leader of the group. I introduced myself to them and asked how many would be coming to Hamilton next year. She said her name was Amina and that she was coming. I told her I would look out for her because I need ninth grade leaders. I made the decision right then that if she came, she would be one of my ninth-grade reps. She did, and has been a leader on campus ever since.

Here's another important point about BSU, or any club that stresses leadership for that matter. In any given year you will have four years of leaders on your campus at the same time. Each grade level has them. It is up to the advisor to seek out and find those leaders, and if you can assemble them all together on one board, or somehow make them your leadership team, then you have something special. That is what we had that year. Each class was strong and they all were committed. The seniors had experienced the state convention and were leaders beyond our school. The juniors and sophomores were just as committed and the freshmen came in ready to lead, but willing to be led. We had assembled a real dream team of leaders on campus. They were all excellent students and they had a real motivation to be examples of that family bond we had established. The seniors and juniors were present that day we had the meeting after the election of 2016. As I said earlier, I believe that meeting laid the foundation for how the BSU students would take care of each other going forward. Now those students were in charge and they not only accepted, but embraced the challenge to be good to each other, to love one another. In my restorative justice circles I would ask the students why it was so difficult to verbally express your love for others, yet so easy to express anger and negative feelings. Even in families where you know the members love each other, it is still often difficult to say. I would ask why that is, knowing there was no easy answer, but I wanted them to think about that. I then decided to model what I wanted, which was the ability to express your love to those you actually love. Since I love my students, among many other people, I decided to tell them. Justin was in some of my circles and brought some of the restorative practices into our meetings. He began the meetings with mindfulness activities like deep breathing to get everyone grounded in our space, and he followed suit to begin telling his peers he loved them. This caught on in the meetings and it became less awkward and more common to see these feelings shared among students on campus. It was beautiful to see.

We had our usual activities before Club Rush including the Back-to-School Night, which was again successful as we provided a treat this time. My long-time best friend Barry supplied us with his "Pearilicous Pies" to sell. These were small single pies that were like a pear cheese cake and they were delicious. He had taken the recipe from his mother and made it his own. Growing up a few doors down the street I had my share of those treats over the years. As expected, they were a big hit and the perfect fundraiser to get the year started. With Club Rush on the horizon in early September, we were preparing for that and our first meeting after. This time we would be announcing a new event in which we would be participating as part of the UBSUC Southern Region. That was the Welcome Back to School Cookout. This was a new activity brought to the region and Andre played a huge part in its creation. The cookout was to be held in Los Angeles at very popular Kenneth Hahn Park. All the schools in the southern region were invited to attend and that means potentially hundreds of high schools in the vast Southern California area. There is, however, a relatively small percentage of schools with BSU's, and among those, there is a small number that are members of the UBSUC. The goal was to change that. On the one hand we wanted to recruit the schools that had BSU's to join the UBSUC, and also we wanted to help those schools that were trying to start BSU's with that endeavor as well. This was a great way to introduce the BSU's to one another, both students and advisors, so we can build a strong network in the southern region. It was a beautiful day at the park as buses came from different parts of the region, not just Los Angeles. I was joined by Mr. Russell, who was the advisor at Santa Monica High School, on the grill. We took care of the burgers and hot dogs and the students had plenty to eat. They did ice-breakers, played outdoor games, and then assembled for a very interesting discussion on how each BSU was impacting their respective campus. They talked about topics such as access to AP classes, college information, and the relationship with their school site peers of other races. Many members of our Executive Board were present at the cookout and surprisingly, Justin happened to be at the same park at the same time with his family for an outing. He did come over for a while and join his Hamilton family where he was embraced and introduced to the whole group as the Hamilton BSU President to a very nice applause. As the students engaged in conversation a young lady began to speak from the center of the group. She spoke about some of the

Kenneth L. Turner

micro, and not so micro, aggressions she has seen in her AP classes. By their reaction, you could see that the crowd could relate and were definitely affirming and supportive of her comments. That student was our very own Aiyana. I had never heard her speak with such authority in front of such a large group of her peers. She didn't know most of them, but she felt very comfortable in that setting. I could see right then that another leader was emerging.

Bungalow 10 was the room where I visited, where I met Olivia and Denim. Eventually the substitute was replaced and the new teacher allowed us to use the room for our BSU meetings if we wanted to. It was the perfect room for our group. The room was a theater style classroom. There were three rows of seats and each row was elevated higher than the one before it. Each row had about 30 seats and then there was a stage area in front that can seat at least 20 more. We started meeting in B-10 and there was standing room only. You can tell when it was Wednesday at school because in the more congested areas on campus during lunch, it was bare.

For the past two years my lunchtime assignment was to be present on the yard, mainly the quad, where most of the students were congregated

252

during that time. I was able, however, to attend the meetings on Wednesdays and let someone else cover my area. I always felt the need to be at every meeting, and I also wanted to be. There were times this year, especially early in the year that I had to miss a meeting, and when that happened, I was always concerned that I might be needed. Then one day I went into a meeting late. When I walked in the students were engaged in a conversation about mental health in the black community. The students were opening up about issues they, or others they knew, were dealing with. Then there were those who had contacts with mental health professionals that they were sharing. There were tears and hugs and I love you's. I stood there really in amazement because it was really the first time I got to see what the meetings were like when I wasn't there. I realized then that this group didn't need me. They had arrived at a point where everything needed to run a successful BSU was there. I then began to think about all the other times in this very early school year where they took the initiative to do something that I had grown accustom to doing. When it was time to submit the paperwork for Club Rush, for example, before I could get the paperwork from the leadership class, the BSU leaders brought it to me for signature.

They had already filled everything out. They did the same when it was time to plan for our homecoming activities, which were securing our spot for tailgate and arranging what we would do for fundraising. When they had their meetings they ran like clockwork, and the room was full, often there was nowhere to stand. They started having meetings on Tuesdays to discuss the topic for the Wednesday meeting. I would sit in on those to see how they decided. There were students who would suggest topics and they would discuss each topic and vote if necessary. Usually a topic would resonate with the whole group as the one and that became the topic for the discussion. A student did not have to be on the board to make a suggestion for a topic. A member could talk to me or anyone on the board at any time and suggest a topic for the meeting. The discussions always seemed to be topics the students wanted to talk about. Justin would start the meeting, but any leader could lead the discussion, and I would always have some opinion, or some way to send an encouraging message or affirmation to the group as my contribution. What I enjoyed most was to see the genuine happiness to reconvene every week. I likened it to going to a family reunion every week.

Soon after Homecoming week it was again time for the UBSUC Southern Region Conference. This time the host school would be Cal Poly San Luis Obispo. This was set to be a long day. The conferences were only one day and the last one was at Cal State Northridge, but because that one was so close it was sort of like a school day only it was a Saturday. For this one we had to meet at Hamilton at about 5:30am and we would not return to the school until about 6pm. The good thing was the fact that we got to sleep on the bus. On this trip I took Andre, as he was a major part of the program as the 1st Vice President of the Southern Region. The other students were all going to their first UBSUC conference and all of them would be running for office for the first time. The other three officers, Deborah, Savannah, and Elisha were all taking the SAT that day and could not make the trip. Aiyana was going to be running for President. There were two other BSU students who I had gotten to know pretty well during their sophomore year last year. Their names were Sharee and Aleisha. While they were taking a World History class they came and shared with me their concern that there wasn't enough black history being taught in the class and that we should have that be more a part of our BSU meetings. I wasn't against the idea.

255

My only concern was that I did not want to make our meeting like going to class. I did want the students to learn more about black history, and I would always challenge them to learn more. I conceded to the two young ladies that they simply were not going to learn much about black history in class, but that did not excuse them from learning about black history if they truly wanted to. There absolutely should be more culturally relevant material taught in all classes, especially history. I also believe that there is so much literature on the black experience that a student can gain a wealth of knowledge and perspective just by reading on one's own. I told Sharee and Aleisha that I would see who else felt the same about BSU sharing more about black history and then I recommended a book to get us started. That book was *Before the Mayflower,* by Lerone Bennett, Jr. I was assigned to read this book when I was a student at Los Angeles Southwest College taking an African American History class. It was the most informative and comprehensive text I had ever read on our history up to that point, and it set me on a course of reading everything I could find on black history. Over the next several years I accumulated an extensive library of books at my home. At first I too wondered why I didn't learn any of this in high school. Then I reasoned that to truly learn information like this there has to be classes in the curriculum just for this material. It cannot be a unit or chapter covered in a text book. What I also know is we cannot wait for others to teach us what we want to know about ourselves. If one can read, the material is there. Sharee was going to be running for 1st Vice President, replacing Andre since seniors were not able to run. Aleisha had decided to run for Parliamentarian. Olivia was running for 2nd Vice President. Another freshman named Eniyah was going to be running for Secretary. Eniyah was part that amazing group of freshmen who had that special spark and she was one of the brightest stars. She was a natural born leader and it came so easy for her to lead her peers that I don't think she understood she had this extraordinary gift. It was her ability to communicate and her comfort level when talking with her peers, even older peers. For Treasurer and Sergeant at Arms our candidates would be Amina and Denim, respectively.

We arrived at Cal Poly San Luis Obispo just as the conference was getting started. We had a light breakfast and then Andre and the President began the program. We were welcomed by one of the school's leaders, and then an inspirational message from a Professor of African American

Studies. The students were then escorted to another building where the workshops were to take place. After the workshops we were provided lunch and then given a tour of the university. The conclusion of the tour led us to the hall where the student candidates would be giving their speeches. To my surprise, of the seven positions available, only three of them had multiple candidates. This was interesting to me because from the beginning my goal was to have a candidate run for each position and I guess I thought other schools had similar goals for their students. The three students who would be running against competition were Sharee, Olivia, and Eniyah. Even when students were called from the floor to run at that time no one decided to run for the other four positions, and so our students would receive the votes necessary to win. When the election was over and it was time to announce the winners. It happened that Sharee was the only one who did not win. The 1st Vice President position went to a very formidable candidate and impressive student from the Santa Maria area named Navy. That meant that of the seven positions on the board, six would be occupied by Hamilton students, including the new President Aiyana. What was even more impressive was that three freshmen won. What this told me was that Hamilton's BSU would be in very good hands going forward, as would our standing in the UBSUC. Just like the year before when we were there to support Aliah and Taylor after they didn't win their positions, here the students were to pick up Sharee. I made sure to let her know how proud I was that she ran and did very well, especially with this being her first experience in the UBSUC.

Soon after the conference those newly elected leaders would join with other board members and other BSU's for our Southern Region Roundtable discussion with Congresswoman Karen Bass. The congresswoman graciously accepted a request to come to speak to the UBSUC Southern Region in this event which was hosted by Loyola Marymount University. There were BSU's from the Santa Maria area in the northern most part of the region all the way to the Long Beach area to the south. The students again had organized the day and followed the program which consisted of peer discussions of articles they read. These articles would be the basis of Congresswoman Bass's presentation. One of my favorite memories about this roundtable was seeing the students from all the schools networking, exchanging information and getting to know each other. Then there was Eniyah playing a lead role in her small group discussion facilitating the conversation with her peers who certainly didn't suspect she was only in the ninth grade. When Congresswoman Bass arrived, she walked into the room to a standing ovation and then took her seat right in the middle of the Hamilton student section. They were extremely proud to know that she was a Hamilton alumnus and I hoped she was as proud of them for the way they represented her alma mater. She talked about what it was like working in congress and the various committees she was on. She urged them to get involved in public service and the importance of what they were already doing as BSU members and members of the UBSUC. She was funny and relatable and all the students learned a great deal that day.

Though my office is always open to students who want or need to talk about their concerns, I look forward to when the bell rings to go out and be among the students during nutrition or lunch. I get to go where they hang out and share a few laughs with them, and because we have so many students, I walk around and visit small groups of them during this time. I take this time to check in and this is really a great way to build community. It is what I have always done. I like to see the students when they are in their element, when they are most comfortable. I think more educators should do this because it helps them see us in a different light. This is what I mean when I say we must "walk this high school journey" with them, day by day. My BSU students and I look forward to seeing each other every day and no matter what the day may bring, I am there. If I am not there and they need to speak with me, they know how to get in touch with me. They may not need lots of attention all the time, but any one of them may need lots of attention at any given time. More than anything I want them to know that I am here when needed. When I walked outside this particular year, I found myself gravitating more and more to the spot where the freshmen hung out. They had such positive energy and I loved being around them. I was spending as much time with them as I was with the other classes because I wanted them know very early on in their high school career that I was going to be there for them and with them. Two more students in that freshman group who began to capture my attention were Cameron and Madisyn. They attended the same middle school as Denim and Eniyah. They were all close friends and I can honestly say that every time I visited their area, which was a bench along the north side of the quad, I felt that love and positivity. Cameron was a biracial student, black and filipino, with a beautiful smile and a humble and sincere nature. She loved to laugh, but when she was serious, or had something on her mind, found it very easy to talk to me. We would talk outside or she would visit my office. We established a great rapport and it kind of reminded me of my relationship with Kenya. Madisyn was a very friendly, virtually impossible to dislike, southern girl from Georgia. She was soft-spoken, and like Cameron, loved to laugh. She was very serious about her education, and yet as down-to-earth as any young student I knew. I later found out there was a fifth member of this lively group that came to us from Burroughs Middle School. Her name was Krista. It took a little longer to get to know Krista because she had more interests outside of school, and then I heard her sing. With a voice like Krista's she probably spends a lot of time in the studio or traveling. She is that good, and we could all see it from a young age. She would eventually carve out a place in our BSU's story for the way she has blessed us all with her talent over her four years. This group would be a foundational piece of our BSU during that time.

By now we had five of our past Presidents or VP's attend UCLA and several more who were not on the Executive Board. Jai, Camille, and Dou'jae were the Presidents and Chantel and Simone were the VP's. This year I knew we had more students on the board and in our family who were applying, and now it was time to take them to the school for our annual Buddy Day trip. Once again we were greeted by the UCLA students and among them of course were Chantel and Jolen, but this time joining them with enthusiasm were Simone and Zeyna who everyone remembers from the year before at Hamilton. When it was time for the students to disperse I saw that Justin had partnered with Jolen and these were two of the most outstanding young men that I have had in BSU. I was proud to get a picture of them as they would symbolize and epitomize the BSU young man at Hamilton. The family has such a large ratio of girls to boys that it sometimes overshadows the fact that we have had some outstanding young men come through our BSU. Some have been on the Executive Board but many have not, nonetheless they have been exceptional and I want to make sure I give them mention here. There are too many to name individually, but in each class I have worked with young men in our BSU that I am extremely proud of. They have served in the highest office in our BSU and in various committees. If you are reading this book and you are one of my guys over the past

12 years, please know how proud I am to have worked with you. One of the best things about this trip was that Kenya was able to attend. Kenya had spent the first two years after she graduated attending UC Riverside. In her third year, however, she transferred to the University of Arizona where she would eventually graduate. Because she was attending school online, she was able to work at Hamilton. Now I had my son there as a student and my daughter as a colleague. That just added to an already great year. And then there was the unexpected phone call. I received a call from Dr. Ernest Black at California State University, Los Angeles, my alma mater, informing me that I had been nominated for a special award. Each year the Charter College of Education awards a Distinguished Educator Award to educators who have impacted the profession and/or students on a large scale, and that have made a huge difference in the community. What made this so special for me was that it was for my work with the BSU. It was not for anything I did in the classroom as a teacher, but it validated and affirmed the time and energy put into this amazing group of young people I've been blessed to work with over the years. Interestingly enough, when you are engrossed in the work, it's easy to overlook things like impact.

You just kind of lose yourself in the service and in the relationships. There is hardly time to step back and reflect. There is always an activity or meeting to plan, a plan to execute, a student who needs help, a conflict to resolve, or decisions to make. I did receive the award along with several other very worthy recipients for the work they had done, and I was so grateful that my father and my children were there with me at the awards dinner. In my speech I emphasized the importance of a loving and caring man in the life of a child. That is what my dad has always been for me, and that is what I have always wanted to be because I have seen the difference it can make. This award was truly one of the highlights of my career. It was around that time that I happened to run into a parent in the hallway at school one day. Ms. Enciso-Givhan was the mother of one our BSU stars and an amazing dancer named Kai. I had met her before, but on this day we stopped and talked for a while and she got an update on how things were going with the BSU. As we talked, she confirmed something that I had thought about periodically, but became clear in this conversation. She told me I should write a book.

Even though it was a great year for BSU, and it was still only the first semester, it was not without its challenges. There was an element of violence and gang activity that I had not seen at Hamilton and that sometimes brings challenges to a BSU because the club is often seen as the "answer" or "remedy" to at-risk behaviors. I have heard many parents and even staff members suggest to a student, "He should get involved in a program like BSU to keep his mind on something positive." I have heard statements like that many times. The problem is as good as that might sound, and it can even be true, a student has to truly *want* something different. BSU is a great option for those who *want* to be around a different group, and away from the gang element. The truth is that some students have absolutely no interest in a club like BSU, and you cannot make them. There may actually be better clubs suited for students who have different interests. For example, there are male only clubs and more hobby-based clubs like weightlifting clubs that some students may find more appealing. Our BSU emphasizes self-control and self-responsibility, and challenges students to become the best version of themselves, and that's in spite of the constant battles in which we find ourselves. That requires a mind that is at least open to that type of thinking. The students who embrace that philosophy tend to not only join, but really get involved in BSU, but admittedly some of our students take longer than others to get there.

Our meetings have been fantastic this fall semester and it was only fitting that we would finish 2018 with the last meeting being our alumni meeting. December is usually the time of year when our students who have gone away to college are back in town. I decided we would have a special meeting dedicated to having alumni come back and share their experiences in college and encourage their younger peers still at Hamilton. Once again all I had to do was tell the board what I wanted and they executed perfectly. They had developed questions from the group so they could maximize the thirty-minute meeting with the alums. They were asked questions like "What was your most memorable experience in BSU?" And there were others that caused them to reflect on those days. It was such a great meeting. The guests who were able to make this special meeting were Simone and Zeyna from the class of 2018, Kenya and Deion from 2016, Mr. Tolson from 2012, Erika from 2013, and Francis from 2017. It felt so good to see the alumni come back and the way they were received confirmed for me that this would be an annual meeting going forward.

Throughout the month of November, I had been in contact with a company called HBCU Hub who was hosting HBCU Night at the Staples Center. Several high schools were invited to attend a panel discussion with alumni from HBCU's who were either entrepreneurs, or worked in various industries including entertainment. After the panel the students were given tickets to the Clippers game. This turned out to be an all-day event on a Sunday, but it was a lot of fun. I took about 45 students to this event. They all enjoyed the very informative panel and had a lot of questions, mostly about life at an HBCU, but a lot about the careers as well. I was able to enjoy time with Isaiah, who brought his friend Robbie from another school. After the discussion we all walked across the street to enjoy pizza at Tom's Urban in LA Live before heading back to the game.

Before the first semester ended, I got a preview of what the BSU Show was going to be about. The students decided they would do a tribute to the role that historically black colleges have played in shaping and advancing black culture over the years. Our newest BSU t-shirts had Hamilton BSU in what can be described as a "Different World" type font, just like the television show, and since the show focused on life at an

HBCU, I think all that served as motivation for our show. They didn't share that with me, nor did I ask, but I absolutely loved the concept, and it made sense if the shirt sparked some interest in a show theme. If you add that we just participated in HBCU Night at Staples Center, it seemed clear that the students had the motivation for this show, which they titled, "A New Step." With the concept clear in December, they began the task of writing the script, which went on through the break. They planned to hold auditions when we came back to school in January. This is the blueprint we typically try to follow when doing the show. Sometime between Thanksgiving and the Christmas break is when the show topic or theme will have been decided. When we return, the focus is always on the show, and inevitably we get caught off guard that first week and never seem to have a solid plan for celebrating Dr. Martin Luther King, Jr. Day. Over the years that is one area where we have fallen short, and if I could improve on anything we do, it would be to have a consistent celebration of King day.

By the time our annual Greek Week and Pan African Film Festival dates rolled around, the students were in full rehearsal mode. I would see Virginia around campus, sometimes tired, sometimes sick, and other times both. She was working very hard with the choreography. As I stayed after school to watch some of the rehearsals, I developed a deeper appreciation for the work of a choreographer. This was the only aspect of the show that I saw during rehearsals because the dancers could not be in the rehearsal room without an adult present. These rehearsals can be so tiring that when we have the opportunity to break for events like the Pan African Film Festival, those days are always appreciated, and this year was no different. The movie of choice this year was *The Hate U Give*. This story seemed to illustrate everything that had been going on over the past few years in terms of racial profiling and the use of force against unarmed black men by police officers, and the feelings about, and the response to these activities by the black community. It was important for Isaiah to see this movie, as it makes one think really hard about police interactions, and for an African American teenager who had not encountered the police in any way, he needed to see what can happen. We had some meaningful conversations after seeing the movie together. This was also when I realized just how much of a trigger that uniform really is to some students. The walkouts, protests, and emotional meetings that we have held definitely spoke to a level of activism in my students, which always impressed me. I felt like this is what we want in our students, to care, to have a vested interested in the things that are going on in the world around them. After seeing this movie, and our subsequent debriefing session, I realized that the uniform, that badge and that gun are real triggers that cause an emotional reaction in some students. It's great to have a culture where students feel safe and can talk about these feelings with their peers.

Last year the Yard Show took our annual Greek Week festivities to another level and raised the bar for years to come. Unfortunately, as good our guests were this year during the classroom visits during the week, we did not get to have our Yard Show due to scheduling conflicts of the college students. I was so disappointed, as I wanted to make sure we held the event every year, but this year it was not to be. We did not have time to dwell on it though because the BSU Show was quickly approaching. When we got to the all-day rehearsal the day before, Kenya played a huge role in assisting with the directing of the show, as there were many moving parts that day. There were lots of scenes and those who were trying to put it all together needed the help of someone who was

271

experienced in how we did the shows. Of course there were those tense moments as there always are, but by the end of the day they were ready. The show took the theme of a young man entering into his freshman year as a new student from California enrolling in a HBCU. The show took the audience through things like meeting his dorm mates for the first time, each one acquiring a nickname. We saw skits on what some of the classes might have been like, and how this student began to embrace this new environment. We saw scenes from the student union where there was poetry night, and we even saw the fraternities and sororities strolling at the party. Our new student, "T--chala" showed great appreciation for what he learned throughout the course of the show including his new friends, historical African American figures, college life, and the appreciation of the unity fostered in such an environment. The dance finale showed the talent and creativity of Virginia, as she had many dancers on the stage going through the choreography, and not all of them were dancers. What was most impressive to me is how she got all of them to work together and put on an amazing performance. She got them to give their all, and as I sat back and watched, that is what these students do. I saw it in Treniece's script writing, with the help of Justin and Aiyana, I saw it in the passion of the spoken word pieces, I saw it in how hard the actors worked to remember lines. When it is time to display the talents of the BSU on stage, they take it very seriously and give their all, and it shows, and it is amazing to witness. It is the manifestation of being a part of something bigger than one's self.

Everyone knows how excited I get when alumni come back and visit. It's always this feeling of when your children go off to college and they come home for the holidays. Whenever they visit campus, if I am around students, which is almost all the time, I have them say a few words of encouragement to their younger brothers and sisters. I sometimes even do what I call surprise Facetime drop-ins where I might have someone in my office, and during the conversation I might be led to call a random former student who is in college, so the student can get to see college taking place in real time at the moment. It usually happens when a student shares with me a college or major they are interested in. I have called former students and caught them walking to their dorm donned with the university shirt, or maybe they just got out of class and had a break, or even in an Uber on their way to take care of business or to see a friend. In addition to the connection and sharing

273

between current and past students, it also keeps my connection with the alumni strong. Quite often this is also done by just a phone call check-in to see how things are going. When I got such a phone call from Aretha this particular year, I was really excited to hear from her. The fact that social media, which I do not have by the way, makes it so easy for people to stay in touch allows me to get news that I would not otherwise get. Kenya, who follows Aretha on Instagram, informed me that Aretha was voted Miss Clark Atlanta University. I was ecstatic. Because of our communication I knew she was very busy on campus. She was involved in numerous extra-curricular activities and despite that was excelling in the classroom. I did not know the process by which they choose a campus queen at the HBCU's, but I do know that they got it right with Aretha. When she called and said she was in town, we arranged for her to speak with about 50 of our top BSU juniors that year. Aretha spoke to them for about an hour, sharing her experiences at Clark Atlanta. These students were freshmen during Aretha's year as BSU President. I was so glad that they can see what became of her after she graduated. We cannot overstate what this does in the mind of young students. Aretha was the second campus queen that we have had in our BSU.

When we went back to UCLA for our sophomore Buddy Day trip, several of our BSU students had heard the word that they had been accepted into UCLA. Three of our Executive Board members, Justin, Deborah, and Virginia, all got in, as did BSU members Mariam and Layla. This was the most that we had get into UCLA in one year since I started with the BSU. I remember the day they found out the news and the text messages I received. It was an amazing afternoon for sure. This trip to UCLA was supposed to be the time when Isaiah got his first chance to go. He had been to the campus before, but unfortunately, he could not make this trip because he had an important test to make up at school. Our next event was a nice contrast to this trip because it highlighted the fact that there are those students who are on a different career path than those striving to go to a university directly out of high school. I have had students who got accepted into multiple universities, but decided they wanted to go to a community college first. This is often a very mature decision the students make. Sometimes it is for financial reasons because some of our students may not qualify for financial aid, but still their parents can't afford to pay the costs. They reason that this saves the family money and they know they are planning to complete the community college requirements and transfer to the university anyway. Sometimes students make the decision to go community college because they know in their heart they are not ready, not mature enough, not disciplined enough to go straight into the university. This is another common conversation that I have with my students, and the self-awareness often impresses me. Other students may not have college in their plans as they seek to learn a trade, go to the military, or have other talents and entrepreneurial interests. For this group I had the opportunity to invite Captain Brent Burton of the Los Angeles Fire Department to come and speak to a group of students, and this turned out to be something many students appreciated. Captain Burton was able to draw the interest of many students by sharing a wealth of information about what firefighters actually do on a daily basis. All the students knew was that they are called to put out fires, and of course they see the trucks when there is a car accident. They were educated on many things they had not considered, including the pay. Several of the students came away from this presentation wanting to join the fire department, or planning to take the steps right away to join. We emphasize scholarship as one our principles, but we also emphasize service, and this is one great way to serve humanity and make a good living without going directly into a university. For BSU advisors, as often as you can get people from various careers to speak with your students, I encourage you to take advantage of it. They will appreciate your efforts to provide them with choices in life. When we celebrate our seniors by posting their picture and college choice on the wall, or on our website, I am sure to post the community colleges and vocational schools as well.

This year's UBSUC State Convention was hosted by the Central Region and it was to be held in Bakersfield. The host school was Cal State University, Bakersfield and the hotel was the Bakersfield Marriott. This was another road trip and we were all excited once again. Once again we would be traveling with Venice High School's BSU, the only other LAUSD school going. We increased our Hamilton group from nine students the year before to twenty-four this year. The students sold popcorn to finance their cost of the trip. They had to raise $250 and if they didn't meet that with the popcorn sales, they had to pay the difference. Hardly any students had to pay anything out of their pocket. Four of the students, the state officers, had their rooms comped so their popcorn sales went to the group. It worked out perfectly and we were set to go. Justin, Andre, Domo, and Myles were the only boys on the trip. We had five rooms with four girls each, and then there was me. This year we were fortunate to have two moms attend the trip with us. Aiyana's mom, Ms. Hall and Mrs. Shinn, the parent of the twins joined us as chaperones and they were fantastic the entire weekend. We had a good mix of our leaders from all grade levels, just like I wanted it. The seniors were Aliah, Elisha, Savannah, Deborah, Aniya, Ericka, Ali, and Treniece. The juniors were Aiyana, Sharie, and Aleisha. The sophomores were Sierra, Olivia, and Korley. I had met Korley after school one day when I responded to a radio call in one of our girl's bathrooms. There was a girl who was really sick in there and Korley had stayed with her until someone came. When I talked to her about what happened, or what she saw, I could see the concern on her face, and how she genuinely cared about this student who she really didn't know. I was impressed with Korley's heart, and I could see that she would make an excellent addition to our board, which she did join later as 11th Grade Rep. The freshmen who came to the convention were Denim, Eniyah, Cameron, Amina, Madisyn, and Soraya, another freshman that I had gotten to

know, who showed great interest in BSU. She
didn't have a particular group that she hung
around, but she did know the freshman going on
this tip. I was glad she wanted to go with us. It had
been my preference to take multiples of four
students because the rooms were more expensive if
there were less than four to a room. It was another
great weekend for our students. The six students
did a great job with their speeches during the
delegate assembly. They got a chance to hang out
at the pool during the two-hour break. Deborah
received the UBSUC Scholarship, and after the
banquet they all enjoyed themselves at the evening
dance. It was announced that Saturday night that
for the second consecutive year Hamilton High
School was voted BSU of the Year. When the
winner was announced, Justin and I looked at each
other with the biggest smile. I was so happy for the
students, and also very proud of them. I reflected
back to the previous year when the board was
being assembled. I saw how those students
impacted the school, and then later, when that
awesome freshman group arrived, I knew this
would be a special year. Yes, we did participate in
a lot of activities, but the bond that was built took
place in the meetings and the interaction and
energy on campus on a daily basis. This was the

year that I felt our BSU had become what I had always envisioned it could be. We had great leadership. They all embraced our core principles of scholarship, leadership, and service. They had a tremendous impact on the school culture and the BSU had just as tremendous an impact on the lives of the students. And they loved each other. All that would run through my mind on the bus on the way home. We still had to wait to see who won their respective positions on the advisory board. When it was time to announce the winners on Sunday, of the six Hamilton candidates we learned that four would be victorious. Aiyana became the new President, and our first to serve as Southern Region and State President. Amina was voted as Treasurer, Denim was voted as Sergeant at Arms, and Aleisha was voted as Parliamentarian. Once again four of seven positions on the state board went to Hamilton students, and then it was time for the outgoing officers to say their goodbyes. This was quite an emotional moment for me as I sat there and listened to what Andre, Deborah, Elisha, and Savannah had to say about their experience with the UBSUC, Hamilton's BSU, and our relationship. Again, when you're doing the work you don't often get to think about things like impact. They let me know my impact that night.

It was time now to begin filling positions on the Executive Board for next year. I had decided to add a few positions this year to make our board more like the UBSUC board. To do this, I added a second VP position, a Parliamentarian, and a Sergeant at Arms position. When we fill the 9th Grade Rep positions that would total 23 students on our Executive Board. The President would again run unopposed and it was primarily for the same reason as Justin did. Aiyana had proven herself as the best candidate and everyone else already decided they wanted her to be the President. She still had to go through the interview process, which she did an outstanding job with, but we had our President and we were excited about it. The two Vice Presidents were Myles and Taylor. We had lots of interest in the open positions on the board this year, and they were filled with some really outstanding and qualified students. The new additions were extremely intelligent and perfect fits for their new roles. For example, the new Secretary was Megan who, like some of the others, had been on every BSU Honor Roll since 9th grade. She was very mature and responsible and when she told me she wanted to be Secretary, I knew we had what we needed. The new Treasurer was Sarah. She had also just become the new Student Body

President. I knew she would be a great addition to our board because she was an outstanding student and leader and always willing to help. Our new Financial Secretary was Hailey, another great addition and together with Megan, she was also a leader of our Humanities small learning community. Aleisha had just won the position of Parliamentarian on the UBSUC board and now she would have the same position on the BSU Executive Board. The new Sergeant at Arms was Kendall who was one of the top students in her class. Cameron would take over duties as our Historian and the new Social Media Coordinator was Juan. He had always been one to help out when needed and when these positions opened, he told me he wanted to be more involved in the BSU activities, and he was welcomed to the board. Olivia had decided she no longer wanted to be a grade level representative. She had developed a particular interest in the BSU Show and wanted to be part of the production team, so I gave her the job, which opened up a position as 11th Grade Rep. That position was filled by Korley. The two students chosen to help Olivia with the show were Noelle, a talented spoken word artist and creative writer and Olivia Blevins, an experienced dancer and choreographer with our dance team. The board was coming together very nicely. For the committee chairs, I chose Janae to lead the Community Service Committee. Janae was a junior, an outstanding student and leader, and someone who had been on my radar since she entered her freshman year. I was informed by a fraternity brother who taught Janae in middle school that this amazing student would be heading our way to Hamilton. He wanted me to look out for her. When I met her I was sure to let her know the connection I had with her former teacher. She didn't need much from me though. Her parents and those who prepared her for high school did an outstanding job. It was clear from day one that this student was destined for success. She had the work ethic, the maturity, and the focus. She was already Junior Class President and she would be the perfect chair of our Community Service Committee. Denim would become the chair of the Fundraising Committee and Sierra would lead the Social Activities Committee along with another new addition to the board named Kelly. Sierra would double as 11th Grade Rep with Korley, and the 10th Grade Reps were Amina and Eniyah. This gave us four of that amazing freshman group who would be leaders on the Executive Board. Though there were many new faces and students I was just getting to know, I felt really good about our leadership going into the next year. I thought it was very comparable to last year's board and I could not wait to see what they would do in the following year.

I decided I would go to the prom again. I had so much fun the year before, and I was very close to these seniors as well. I had been invited to several pre-prom parties, but I had to be at the prom at a certain time, since I would be chaperoning. I decided to go two parties. Both were not far from my house so I could go to both and then make it to the prom on time. First I stopped by Chante's Champagne Party. I could not miss this one because Chante was my assistant in the office this semester, and also she was the third, and youngest sister of Keara and Jai, who were foundational pieces of the BSU. I saw both sisters and many other BSU alumni, but the star of the show was Chante. She looked beautiful. I remembered meeting her when she was still in middle school, and here she was now about to graduate. When I left there, I stopped by Dominic's house where he and Andre were there with their dates. They would be riding to the prom together. My two guys looked as cool as can be and they were definitely ready for a good time. It was great to see their parents as well as Chante's parents. By now I felt like part of the family. We all had a great time that night. The students deserved it.

It had been nine years since I began this journey with our BSU and every graduating class was special. Each year the BSU leaves a lasting impression on the Hamilton community and you can tell that by the anticipation of the students coming in to each year. Senior Awards Night brings the end of the year front and center. It's usually held about a week before graduation so on that night we knew the big day was right around the corner. Our Outstanding Scholar Award went to Deborah, and the Outstanding Leadership Award to Justin, both on their way to UCLA. Ali was awarded the Commitment to Service Award, which she deserved and would take that to Berkeley with her. The two students who were my clear choice for the BSU Award of Excellence were Andre and Aliah. For four years they were pillars of the BSU and had a hand in every moment of success and achievement we experienced during that time. Aliah would go on to UNLV the following year, and Andre's path took him to the community college. It was now time to say goodbye to this class and I knew it would be emotional. I didn't know how or why even, but I

285

felt the emotion would somehow get the best of me. The graduation was at the Greek Theater in Los Angeles, the perfect venue for a large graduating class. This outdoor concert venue is surrounded by mountains covered with green foliage which serves as the backdrop for the red seats and concrete-colored benches as you move further back from the stage, which has two very large screens flanked on either side that make seeing the stage from far back very easy. Our graduates wear green caps and gowns and with the Kente cloth sash of our BSU students along with the other cords they adorn makes this scene a beautiful tapestry of excellence. I sat on stage during the ceremony and took it all in as I looked out at the crowd as the speakers came up before the graduates were announced, the moment everyone waited for. It started for me when Justin was called to walk across the stage. He unzipped his gown and flashed his BSU t-shirt he was wearing underneath. He *was* BSU, and he wanted everyone to know it as he crossed the stage. I could feel the emotion rising. For years now, the Hamilton community and my colleagues knew the mutual love and affection I had with the BSU students. When he showed his shirt everyone knew how I would feel. I kept it together though for the rest of the ceremony, but when it was over and everyone began to make their way around to take pictures with their friends and family, several students came to the stage to thank administrators and those of us who were there. When Aniya came to the stage we gave each other a big hug, and then it happened. I felt her body begin to sort of tremble from the emotion she was feeling and I heard her crying, and then my emotions finally gave way to the moment and I began crying with her. She had done it. Aniya had always shown me such a great deal of respect and admiration and I loved her fun-loving spirit. I felt everything she was trying to say and I told her I loved her too. It was a very special moment. She too would be on her way to UNLV and I was so proud of her. By the time we finished our hug other students, namely Justin and Andre and a few others came around but I could hardly stop crying. They looked at me with smiles and all I could say is, "You don't understand." What did I mean? They didn't understand how grateful to God I was to have them in my life, and how much I truly loved them. That is what I was feeling. When I finally pulled myself together, I made my way out to the front and took pictures with as many BSU students, (and others), as I could find. The last picture I took was of Aliah as I made my way to my car. Her family, who I had known, was so proud, and rightfully so. It is fitting that the last picture I got of this class was with her, the symbol of everything BSU was...scholarship, leadership, and service wrapped together in the covering of a beautiful family.

10
When the Music Stops (Keep Dancing)

The Associated Student Body (ASB) class at Hamilton is a student-led teacher-sponsored class which serves as the student government or leadership class. In the past it had been combined with the senior class leadership to form one class. The difference is that the ASB students schedule activities and works to serve the student body as a whole. The senior class students focus specifically on senior class activities. Going into the 2019-20 school year the decision was made to separate the two classes and have a teacher for each. A lot of the leg work for both classes over the past two years had been done by a former BSU student, Deion, who graduated in 2016. Currently attending Cal State University, Northridge, Deion worked at Hamilton and provided lots of assistance to the teacher. This year, however, with the separation of classes, I had been given the task of taking over the ASB class, which I soon realized significantly increased my workload. I was now Restorative Justice Coordinator, BSU Advisor, and ASB Sponsor. Keep in mind BSU was not an actual full-time job, except at Hamilton High School, and there still was no pay, though it has never been about the pay anyway. I was now meeting the ASB students every 5th period and several of them were also BSU students, including the Student Body President, Sarah and the Junior Class President, Janae. My first priority with ASB students was to set a culture of selflessness. I told them they are a "collection of leaders working *with* other people, *on behalf* of other people." I believed that for the class to thrive they had to embrace the idea of serving the school. It was not about what they wanted individually, but about the school. We had always had at least a few BSU leaders in ASB, but now that was magnified by the fact that I was ASB Sponsor. My goal was to make sure that there was no sign of a conflict of interest. When I was in ASB, BSU was just another club like all the rest and held to the same rules and guidelines as all the others. Within BSU we always knew we had a governing body (ASB) whose rules and guidelines we had to adhere to, so there would be no issues of conflict. This was one of the first conversations I had with Aiyana and the new Executive Board coming in to the year.

Early registration was always a good time to meet the new incoming students and this year several of the clubs decided to come out and greet the newcomers. We had a BSU table set up so students could ask questions about the club and possibly sign-up before school started, avoiding what was sure to be a long line during Club Rush. By now it was pretty common that students would enroll in 9th grade already knowing about, and seeking out our BSU. I credit a lot of that to Family Day and the families that come through, where younger siblings hear a lot about BSU at home. In our first Executive Board meeting two weeks into the school year, I notified the board that 99 freshmen had signed up for BSU during early registration. This was by far the most freshmen we had sign up, but in fairness it was our first time with a table during early registration, and there would be more at Club Rush.

The UBSUC Southern Region leaders had once again planned the Welcome Back Cookout, which means that six of our leaders were hard at work planning this event. Those who had won positions last fall were serving out the last few months of their term until the elections in the Regional Conference in November. The event was held at the same park in Los Angeles, and I am proud of the fact that most of the Executive Board members were present. The day was overcast and actually rained a little bit but it did not stop the networking and the activities to bring more schools into the Southern Region. The leaders facilitated small group discussions. I was paired with Eniyah, who was again awesome in this role. This time as a 10th grader and when that was mentioned to the students, I actually heard one say, "I thought she was a senior." I also enjoyed seeing the students who were new to the board witness the BSU outside of school and their peers lead in this much greater setting.

Back at school we still had to complete our board by adding the two 9th Grade Reps. I had met a student during registration and I remembered her when the time came to fill the position. I did not talk to her or her parents too long but I was impressed with what they shared about her academic strength. She was a very good student, kind of shy, but seemed to be a good fit for our board. Her name was Xolani. I approached her about being on the board and she accepted the position. Later Amina told me she had someone who she thought would be good for us. When she brought Shomari to meet me I was very impressed. He was exactly what I was looking for. We wanted to keep adding boys to the board who were very good students and who wanted to be a part of a positive campus culture. Shomari was very respectful. His teachers were all impressed with him. He was an athlete who played baseball and basketball. Now our board was complete with two outstanding additions.

Club Rush took on a different tone this year. I was not just responsible for our BSU table, but now I was overseeing the planning of the entire event. I could not just station myself at the BSU table anymore. I had to move around and check on everyone. I was also on the microphone on stage promoting the clubs and playing music. We had our partners from Stepping In The Right Direction there with us once again. The students at the BSU table did a great job once again. I could see that I really didn't need to be there. They had it covered. With the increased number of freshmen who signed up for BSU we had now had the highest membership in all my years as advisor. We had reached a total of 547 students. Just like with Club Rush, my role with Homecoming would be different. It wasn't about what we would be selling at tailgate. There were all the Homecoming festivities. It was important that the BSU leadership was strong and ready to execute because I could not provide as much guidance as I had in the past. They were more than ready. They gave shifts to those whose would be working. Aiyana and Paris worked the game shift, selling chicken dinners near the concession stand. The rest of the BSU students enjoyed the Homecoming game as they should.

By the time she reached her second year at UCLA, Simone was already in charge of arranging our Buddy Day trip as our VIPs mentor. I attribute this to her being prepared to lead such a program while she was in high school. I was always proud to work with former BSU students in these roles when they got to college. Deion was another one. While a student at Cal State Northridge he earned a position of overseeing many of the Black student groups on campus. This included setting up Buddy Day for our group. He had learned about a trip like this from his experience in attending Buddy Day while in our BSU. He arranged for us to meet with the buddies at CSUN, shadow them as they go about their day, then reconvene in a nice meeting where there was a panel of students and a Professor of African American Studies. This was the beginning of annual trip we would take to Northridge and it definitely helped change the perception of the school as well as the desire of students to attend. There had already been several Hamilton graduates, specifically from our BSU that were now attending Northridge, and there would be more applying this year. While attending these trips I was in the process of setting up another college trip with the help of another former BSU student, Kaylin. This time we were preparing to visit Cal State L.A. We did not get to visit the school during the first semester, but it was certainly on the schedule for the second semester and I was excited to be taking students to visit my alma mater.

The Southern Region UBSUC Fall Conference this year was to be held at UC Santa Barbara. As the day approached, even on the way there with a new contingent of student leaders ready to make their mark once again, I knew at some point I would have to find a way to reach Donica, a former BSU student in her second year at UCSB. I hoped she would be on campus and would be able to come and see us for a while. UCSB did a fantastic job of incorporating everything we could ask for in the conference. There was a very nice welcome complete with breakfast. The university representatives went out of their way to make sure everyone felt welcome. The workshops had very good speakers and panelists. The BSU students who greeted us and spoke to us as a panel were friendly, authentic, and engaging. They really gave all the high school students present a clear sense of what being a student at UCSB was like and I know my students came away really impressed and intrigued. Fisher and Gregory were two young men that I brought to the conference. They had not attended a UBSUC event before, but these were two young men who I felt were ready to step into leadership roles within our BSU, and it would begin with their participation and exposure to this conference. Gregory's mother, Mrs. Anderson traveled with us to UCSB and it was great to have her present. She was very supportive of our program, and I am sure since it was her first time attending, she came away impressed with what she saw. I did indeed catch up with Donica and she came to spend most of the time in the conference with us. She also participated on the panel.

Aiyana was present to play the lead role as President of the youth advisory board. Fellow officers who had won the previous year were Denim as Sergeant at Arms, who this year would be running for President. Amina, who was Treasurer was present, but she too would be running for a different position this year as Secretary. Cameron, the reigning Parliamentarian would be running for the same position again, and Eniyah, who had been Secretary, was now running for First Vice President. Gregory would be running for Sergeant at Arms, and Fisher was running for Second Vice President. We did not have a candidate for Treasurer this year. To lend the group some additional support, Sierra attended the conference as did Chanel and Alicia. These were two sophomores who were close friends of Denim, Amina, and the rest of the sophomore group. I certainly tried to convince them both to run for positions as well but they just didn't want to, and it really was ok. I always feel a need though to expose them to these opportunities and give that nudge just in case that is what they need to give it a try. The students campaigned hard after they gave their speeches. This time we were the only LAUSD school present, but Santa Monica was there once again. After the caucusing and voting the winners were announced. It turns out that Denim lost in a close race to Navy, who had been extremely impressive since I had met her through these conferences and UBSUC meetings. She was a formidable candidate and it didn't surprise me that she won. I felt really bad for Denim, we all did. We all knew how bad she wanted to be President. However, I knew once the initial shock of it wore off, Denim would be back. It was only her sophomore year, and I think she made her mind up then that the next time she ran for office she would leave no doubt she was the best candidate. We came out of the conference with five students on the advisory board, all of whom would be running for state office at the Spring convention scheduled to be in the Southern region this year, and we decided on Torrance as our location with Cal State Dominguez Hills as our host university.

As the planning of the BSU show began to take shape we still had our upcoming alumni meeting planned for early December. The Social Activities Committee also planned a Karaoke Night that turned out to be really fun. It was actually a Game Night *and* Karaoke Night. We stayed after school and had hot chocolate and played dominoes and other card games. I served as the barista for the night. Then we went upstairs to a larger room and had our time of karaoke. Once again, I heard songs I had never heard before, which usually happens when I am around the students and music is playing, but I truly enjoyed it. The night would not have been complete without Sierra doing a Tupac song. Additionally, I had seen Aiyana act, heard her do spoken word, and had seen her dance. This was the first time I heard her sing. I said to myself, "What *can't* she do?" I thought about getting up and singing, but I just could not decide which Earth, Wind and Fire song to sing, so I passed. Days later we had our annual alumni meeting. This was more of an HBCU theme. Our alumni guests were DeeDee (Nazeema), who now attended Grambling State University; Malik, who attended Miles College in Alabama; Dylan, who attended Fisk University, and Elisha and Luzine who were currently attending community colleges planning to transfer. This time they did not have prepared questions and the meeting took on more of a conversational tone, but I loved having them there. Dylan would later represent Fisk at the annual Black College Expo at the Los Angeles Convention Center. I was so proud of all of them. The thirty-minute lunch meeting, which ends up really being about 20 minutes is way too short to really hear the experiences of the alumni. Nonetheless I appreciate the time they took to visit us staying true to the service model that our BSU holds as a core value. The team came to me and shared that the BSU show would be a tribute to the three founders of Black Lives Matter, Alicia Garza, Patrisse Cullors, and Opal Tometi. The show would take the audience through various scenes depicting the acts of violence against unarmed black people as well as other encounters of blatantly racist behavior. It would include lots of acting parts as well as spoken word and singing. There would be a couple of dance pieces including a dance finale which Olivia would choreograph. The preparation of the show, which was titled "History In the Making" would take us through the Christmas break and into a second semester never to be forgotten.

Our trip to Cal State L.A. took place soon after we returned to school. It was not a Buddy Day trip like the others where we went to classes and had that experience, but we did get to meet members and students of their Pan African department. Kaylin served as one of the hosts. We took a tour of the university and got a chance to eat in the food court before returning back to Hamilton. Since we took different groups of students to each university, we could not have them compare each experience, but I can share that with the Cal State schools there was more of a recruiting component to the trip. Each of the two universities, Cal State Northridge and Cal State L.A. used the opportunity to make their presentation and they both did a good job. The number of applicants from our BSU to both schools has increased over the last few years as a direct result of these experiences.

It had only been three and a half years since she walked across the stage at Loyola Marymount University to receive her diploma with the Hamilton High School Class of 2016. Here she was now about to turn 21 years old just one month after walking across another stage. This stage, however, was in Centennial Hall at the University of Arizona where she received her B.A. degree in Psychology. I was extremely proud of my daughter who graduated in just three and a half years. She decided to spend her 21st birthday in Las Vegas. The morning her mom and I went to pick her up from the airport we received some shocking news. Across all the outlets it was being reported that Los Angeles Laker Kobe Bryant was in a helicopter crash in Calabasas, California and that all the people on board were killed, including his daughter. I was stunned. We continued to listen to the news for more information, but by the time we headed for the airport it was clear that this would be a sad day, and the sadness would last for a long time. The basketball coach in me, the father in me, as well as the fan in me, was just filled with grief. I could not believe what I was hearing. When we got to the airport, Kenya was standing outside waiting, sobbing. I hate to see her cry. I thought about our relationship and how she became this huge sports fan because of my work as a coach. This was too much. This is how 2020 would begin. The tragic death of Kobe Bryant and all the passengers on that helicopter had a tremendous effect on our students, as it did everywhere I am sure. They wore Kobe jerseys to school and anything they had that honored him could be seen all over. It was in this context that we had to push forward with the events of Black History Month.

I was able to reconnect with many of my associates in the Greek community and we did have our annual Greek Week, including the Yard Show finale. This year we had the Alphas, Kappas, and Zetas perform. We also had a Sigma join us on that day as they came to visit the ASB class after lunch. Though there were not as many organizations that showed up, it was still a great show and a really nice turn out by the students. Another one of our activities this month was the HBCU Fair at Charles Drew University in Compton, California. Since many of the HBCU's application deadlines are well into the Spring semester, students still have a chance to apply even as late as July. The California schools usually have their deadlines at the end of November. We had many students who applied to colleges right there at the fair, some got accepted and some were offered scholarship money. All of this was leading to the annual Black College Expo later in the month. Many of those university representatives will arrive in Los Angeles a week or two early and make visits to some of the local high schools. In the past we had such visits from Bethune Cookman University. This time it was Florida A&M University. Our students got a chance to hear directly from the President of the university and the Dean of Admissions. They made a great presentation. The line of communication had been opened and now our BSU had a great connection and access to a remarkable university.

The BSU Show was now upon us and once again it was great to see all the hard work that was put into it. The script was well put together as it took the audience through various scenes beginning with Trayvon Martin. Woven into the fabric of the show were spoken word pieces and a beautiful rendition of the song *Stand Up* by Cynthia Erivo from the movie *Harriett*. The show ended with the three founders represented by Noelle, Olivia H., and Denim giving a last word, and then the dance finale to Kendrick Lamar's *We Gon' Be Alright*. We did four shows that day and rested the last period because for the first time in my role as BSU advisor, and I'm quite sure the first time maybe ever, the BSU Show would run Friday night for the general public. We sold tickets for only five dollars. Our house band gave a mini-concert along with the show. After the night show, which was a huge success, I was surprised that the students presented me with a t-shirt and a really nice picture collage for my 10th year anniversary with the BSU. I could not believe it had been ten years already.

Throughout the whole month the students had been working hard to sell popcorn in order to raise money for the coming UBSUC State Convention. I personally had been preparing also to attend another conference. It was the annual (CAAASA) California Association of African American Superintendents and Administrators Conference in Sacramento, California. Adult and youth board members had attended their roundtable in the fall to promote the UBSUC. This conference was scheduled to take place in mid-March with the UBSUC State Convention just a week later. There had been reports in the news every day about a virus that had originated in China and had reached the United States. It was called the Corona Virus, or Covid-19. It seemed that every day this virus dominated the news cycle. Every day it was being reported that more and more people were dying from the virus that was highly contagious and transmitted through the air. Some of our students started wearing masks to school, and there began to be rumblings of school closures. I didn't think it would come to that. We had been told that the schools might close for two weeks until things got better, but I heard no official word. When the day came to travel to Sacramento to the CAAASA Conference I was very excited. I was going to be speaking in one of the sessions about our BSU, and how BSU's could impact the school and its members, if done right. As I sat in the airport awaiting my flight, I heard people nearby talking about the NBA had cancelled the game between the Oklahoma City Thunder and the Utah Jazz due to uncertainties over the coronavirus. Right then I knew this had to be very serious. If the NBA canceled a game, I wondered at that point would the conference I was about to attend be canceled as well. I boarded the flight and was in Sacramento in about an hour. There was to be a Sacramento Kings game scheduled for that night, but when I arrived, there was no game, nor was there any crowd to speak of. I didn't hear any news of the conference being canceled, and in fact it was not. As one of the presenters, I got a chance to highlight all the ways a BSU can benefit a school culture and impact its members. I spoke to people from throughout the state and the presentation was received very well. I was grateful for the opportunity. When I returned back to L.A. that night, I was anticipating the work that had to be done the next day because I knew the popcorn had arrived and we would be distributing to the students who were going to the UBSUC State Convention. When I got to work, I immediately began going through all the lists separating the bags of popcorn according to which students needed how many bags of each flavor. To my surprise and many others, it was announced that school would be closing that day. This was to be the last day of school for at least two weeks. The day was March 13, 2020, Friday the 13th. The students had to clear out their lockers of important items such as their books and other personal belongings. The teachers, administrators, and those of us who had offices had to do the same. I was also tasked with making sure all the students had the popcorn they needed to distribute to their buyers. It was a surreal day. I could not believe what was happening, but by now I knew this coronavirus was not just serious, it was dangerous. While I was distributing popcorn, the news came to me from the UBSUC President that the state convention was now being canceled. The students still had to distribute their popcorn, but the money raised would now have to be used for something else. Thanks to one particular student we had a solid contingency plan. Myles and Aiyana had approached me earlier about creating a BSU scholarship. He came up with the idea and all the details of how this scholarship was to work during his Ethnic Studies class as a project. This was something I had thought about any way, but Myles put the work into it to make it a reality. We used the popcorn money to start our BSU Legacy Scholarship Fund. For the next few weeks, and there had been no sign that we were coming back after two weeks, I thought we might return after the Spring break, which meant the return date would be April 13. Until then, all there was to do was to check in with my students and await any news from the district. Fortunately, I was on the admin team and therefore kept abreast of any news coming to the schools in our admin meetings. We had to learn how to attend and conduct meetings on Zoom, the platform by which we were to conduct remote meetings and hold our classes while we were away from school. We were given opportunities to learn how to access these digital platforms to teach our classes and remote learning would now be the way in which school was to work moving forward. I started to hold my ASB class on Zoom, and we held our BSU meetings on Zoom as well. It was very strange at first, but we quickly got used to it. Soon after we started meeting on Zoom, Ms. Monroe contacted a friend of hers named Dr. Noelle Reid, who had been on a reality TV show called *Married to Medicine.* Dr. Reid joined our Zoom one evening and gave lots of information about the coronavirus, how it works, and how to stay safe physically and emotionally during this pandemic. She also shared her background with the students including how she got into medicine, and her love for dance. She was the perfect guest for our students. She was relatable, funny, down-to-earth, and really educated us all. The success of that meeting led to an idea about having guests on a regular basis. We would do just that later on.

The two-week prediction along with my after-spring-break prediction had now become over two months out of school and it was clear we weren't going back. The seniors would have to have a remote graduation. The admin team was given the task of taking around yard posters and window posters and delivering them to seniors. I tried to get as many BSU seniors as I could so I could at least see them in person. We had a remote Senior Awards Night in late May and I had to read the winners of the BSU Awards from my living room. It took a few takes but I finally was able to announce the winners. The Scholastic Achievement Award went to Kendall, who had an outstanding year academically, and she would be going to UC San Diego. The Outstanding Leadership Award went to Aiyana, who did just a fantastic job all year as the BSU President. She was headed to Dillard University. The Commitment to Service Award went to Sarah, and after a tough decision she committed to Wesleyan University. The BSU Award of Excellence went to Taylor and Myles. Taylor became another Yankee Bruin by going to UCLA, and Myles went to community college before transferring to Texas Southern

Kenneth L. Turner

University. I felt so bad for this senior class. They didn't get to go to their prom, nor did they have all those special senior moments in person. Their senior year also ended in the midst of nationwide protest.

It was the day after Memorial Day and I got a text message from Sarah as I was watching television on this Tuesday night. The text message read, "Did you see this?" There was also a video with the message showing a man on the ground next to a police car with an officer's knee on his neck. The man was yelling out in agony even to the point of calling for his mother. That man died that day, and that's how I found out about the George Floyd murder. I watched the video several times and just kept shaking my head, growing angrier and sick to my stomach. The murder was on a Monday, but I found out the next day. We had decided to cancel our BSU meeting on Wednesday already, but by Thursday I decided to write a statement and send it to all the BSU students. The statement read:

Students of the Hamilton High School Black Student Union:
I want to send my love and support to you during these uncertain times. Let's start there. As you and

I watch what's going on around the country I cannot help but think about your emotions; what you must be feeling, thinking. Maybe you're mad, sad, afraid, confused, or all of the above. You want answers. You want solutions. You want...justice. Everything you are feeling is legitimate and you are not alone. When this happened in 1992 it changed the course of my life. My response was to affect change by becoming an educator, which led me to you, and you to me, and now look what we have together. My question is how will this change you? When you take some time to think, and always take time to think, what will become of this moment? Your moment. I love you, and I believe in you. You matter. You're not an accident. You're not an inconvenience. You are fearfully and wonderfully made.

Mr. Turner

That statement went out on a Thursday, but even before I sent it, I received a call from our Principal suggesting that we give the students an opportunity to talk a about what happened and the resulting protests that had begun to take place. We decided to schedule two initial meetings on Zoom in the coming days for that purpose. The problem was there had not been a written statement from the school to Black students addressing this issue. Consequently, another statement had circulated throughout the school stating that the school didn't really care about its Black students. This led to a full-on social media assault on many members of our faculty by students present and past citing incidents of racism, perceived racism, racial insensitivity, discrimination, or any synonymous term. There was clearly much anger and much pain communicated on the social media platform, so by the time we had our first meeting with the students and members of our admin team, they were definitely ready to express how they felt. The accusations and insults came quickly and furiously. The voices were loud and the emotion of the moment had clearly taken control. As painful as it was to witness this display, it was important to let the students speak. The meeting was supposed to take place for a specified time because I had a meeting immediately after. When that time came, even I was accused of not letting the students continue to speak. No one was spared. There were those who felt that the adults who were attacked should not be so sensitive because the students were only speaking their truth. Then there were those who felt the students had completely crossed the line and the level of disrespect was uncalled for. I was really conflicted and really saddened by what took place. I did want the students to be able to express themselves, but I didn't like the way they went about it. It was difficult watching people I love, hurt people I love. Some of the accusations related to incidents I knew a lot about, and I knew the facts were being incorrectly stated, but in that setting there was no use trying to explain. Any rebuttal to the accusations brought out more complaints. That meeting would be the only one we had. It was enough, but the social media posts kept coming. During the meeting it was also communicated that a list demands was forthcoming to the administration. When I learned that some BSU students were behind some of the comments, or liking what was being said, I began to wonder if my voice was no longer the voice that needed to lead the BSU. It is simply not the way I lead. I told the students about the dangers of collateral damage and they knew I was not in favor of taking to social media. I had a choice to make in my opinion. If this was the direction they wanted to go as a BSU, then I would respect it and remove myself from my role, clearing the way for someone else to take over, and I was serious. The students also had a choice. They had to decide the type of leadership style they wanted in their advisor. There were students who marched at some of the local protests, carried signs, and even had bull horns, and I loved seeing them out there for a great cause. I encourage them to fight for what they believe in, but I believe in thinking and planning and not being driven solely by one's emotion. Have your facts and make your case, but consider the unintended consequences that may arise. That is how I lead and it has served me well for many years. However, I had to acknowledge that the leader they want and need might need to be someone else. We had just established our new Executive Board, and for the first time, we had a President who was not a senior. Denim was the unanimous choice for BSU President and she too ran unopposed. Once we got the board together, I had to meet with them to see what they wanted and if they were ok with the way I was leading them as their advisor. They all felt that my style was what they appreciated and they wanted me to remain as their leader. At that moment we re-committed to our principles and our bond together. The first thing I wanted them to do was to put out a statement of their own because no one should be speaking for them. They were the BSU. They had the ear of the administration, and the respect of the

Hamilton community. When they released their statement they stated that, "While acknowledging that there are legitimate concerns of black students that need to be addressed, we, the Hamilton High School Black Student Union Executive Board declare that the recent statements regarding a list of demands has no correlation/association with the Hamilton Black Student Union, and that no current active members of the Executive Board were involved in its creation; that Black Student Union is inclusive to students of all races; and that Black Student Union does not support the phrasing of demands." This statement went to the Principal and the admin team and each member of the Executive Board was listed as a signer. When that statement got back to the other student group, they decided to have a meeting. I was in full agreement that they meet, and I was willing to be present, but only if another adult was present. If not, I wanted the two groups to work together on their own. What I did tell the BSU students was that I did not want these two groups, who both had positive intentions that would benefit black students, to be in conflict with one another. When they had the meeting, I was called to join after they had discussed everything. I was pleased and proud to see that they had worked out a peaceful and collaborative solution. That each group had a different way of going about creating change, but there would be mutual respect for the efforts of each going forward. The students reached that agreement without the help of any adults, and that was Denim's first task as President. She exceeded expectations and I knew she was ready to lead the BSU.

We were still in a pandemic. There were still long lines to get into stores, and when you did get in, much of what you needed was off the shelves. There were nationwide protests taking place, and our students were right there demanding justice. Our graduates had to have a remote ceremony. Through it all, however, BSU stood strong, and actually grew stronger in the midst of a very traumatic situation on our campus. That meeting would haunt faculty members for some time, but the BSU looked inside itself and remembered that love and the relationships are the key. It reminded me of the time when our dancers were dancing onstage and the music stopped in the middle of their routine. I told the crowd that there was a lesson in what just happened. "Are you so prepared that when things don't happen the way you want them to, when the music stops, are you prepared to keep dancing without missing a beat?"

They were still a force on campus, and they would continue to be a unifying force for the Hamilton community. A new BSU parent group had been established and it would be led by Lisa Shinn and Jennifer Black, two of the mothers with whom I had worked very closely. Lisa, of course was the mother of the twins Sierra and Skyler, and Jennifer, I met when I took Calvin to the Young Men's Conference. Starting with these two parents we began to build this parent group with more very supportive parents. This important piece had been missing for so long, and it was just what we needed. This group would meet over the summer and become a tremendous support system for me. BSU not only survived the Spring of 2020, but went into the summer full of optimism. We didn't know when we would be returning to school, but what we did know was that BSU would still be going strong no matter what.

.

11

A Model of Resilience

For as far back as I can remember, I have always loved working with children. I have thrived in these mentor/mentee relationships. Before I became an educator, I was a coach, and even then, it was about more than just basketball. Before I became an actual coach of a school's basketball team, I was a counselor for the National Youth Sports Program at the University of Southern California. The official title I held then was counselor because we did more than just teach our team how to play sports. We guided them through a summer complete with athletic competition and enrichment programs. We built relationships. We spent time with our team and we talked. We served as role models, and even then, I was barely twenty years old. I loved the idea that I could have such a positive impact on young people, and they were really only a few years younger than I was. As I held these positions, counselor, coach, teacher's aid, I just knew that I loved the feeling of working with young people. On April 29, 1992 I realized this role had become my purpose. That was the day that the sweeping not-guilty verdicts were read when four police officers were on trial for beating civilian Rodney King. That day I was at work at Horace Mann Junior High School. By the time I got home, about 15 minutes later, I saw helicopters circling certain parts of the city. When I turned on the news, I saw the corner of Florence and Normandie, where the helicopters were gathered suspended in the air showing another civilian, Reginald Denny, getting pulled from his truck and beaten. This was the beginning of the 1992 LA riots, where only steps away I attended a child day care center some twenty-five years earlier. I saw young people just like those with whom I worked every day out in the streets. They were protesting, but they were also looting, burning buildings, and following older people who were doing the same. I sat and watched my city burn for three days, and felt that there had to be something I could do. Then it became crystal clear to me. Teach the children. This was no longer just something I loved doing. It became what I *had* to do. I still loved it, but now it became my mission to do what I could to help young people find happiness, find inner peace, find success, and find…themselves. I could not find these things for them. I could only help them, and the only way I knew how do that was to build relationships, to be there, to be a caring man in the lives that I touched, the same way my dad has always been for me. The satisfaction of seeing these young people succeed, or even have those small victories on the way to ultimate success has become my greatest reward. This is especially true when I see them persevere through difficulties, when I am there with them through the struggles and the low moments, and then I am still there with them when they come out, having grown from those experiences, those moments are priceless. When I got to know Denim, all those feelings were activated.

After we met, she began to come to my office whenever there was something she wanted to talk about. Through these conversations we developed a strong bond. She trusted me and felt a comfort level when coming to me, and I was sure to honor that and to be fully present for her when she needed that. I learned a lot about her during these conversations, but one of the most impressive things I learned was how much she cares for other people. She often came to me about other people who she felt were going through things, and she wanted me to look out for them. She believed I could help, and many of these students never knew that she was advocating for them. Then I began to notice how comfortable she was in settings where she had to speak in front of groups. She was gifted in this area. She had a way of making members of an audience feel as though she were talking to just them. Many of her early presentations were neither written, nor rehearsed. She just talks to people. Her communication skills, her positive demeanor, and her caring nature made her a clear choice for BSU President at the end of her sophomore year. I was concern that it might be too much since we never had a President before who was not a senior. How would her senior peers react? Would she be able to handle the pressure? When I saw that she was unopposed it became even more important than usual that the team around her would have to be a very solid and cohesive unit, and would support her. It was also necessary to select students who could step in when needed to lead the group. We assembled just the right team. Our two Vice Presidents were Amina and Sierra, two long-time BSU members who were both very capable of stepping up to lead the BSU at any time. The Secretary was Janae, who had just been elected as Student Body President, just as Sarah had been the year before. Newcomers to the board were Matthew and Courtney to serve as Treasurer and Financial Secretary, respectively. Matthew and Sierra would join an impressive list of past Yankee Bruins when they made their commitment to UCLA later in the Spring. Courtney, the younger sister of Sharee, had also been a very strong and dedicated member prior to joining the board. Cameron would become our Parliamentarian. Fisher was our new Sergeant at Arms. Another newcomer to the board was Andres, who would serve as our Historian, and Chanel would handle our social media. Chanel was also a school leader serving as our Junior Class Vice President. Andres was a Mexican American student, a close friend to many of our BSU leaders, a true ally of the Black community, and an overall outstanding young man. I got to know Andres years earlier when I facilitated community building circles with his class. He had been a member of BSU since his freshman year. For her second year, Olivia Holley would be our BSU Show Director and this year she chose an outstanding writer and spoken word artist, Jada, to join her. Jada had performed in previous BSU shows as well as many recitals outside of school. She was a very gifted writer, and I didn't understand just how gifted until our BSU show. Korley was selected to serve as the choreographer for our dance pieces, and that completed the production team. The committees would be chaired by Christiana, Community Service; Madisyn, Fundraising; and Dalayna would lead the Social Activities Committee. Our new Scholarship Committee would be led by a senior named Brandon. He was an outstanding student in his own right, and no doubt could have won the BSU Legacy Scholarship, but wanted to serve in this capacity even though it would disqualify him from running. This selfless act symbolized what this group was all about. Also new to the board were juniors Lauren and Aliyah. Both had been very active in BSU and had now become ready to serve on the board. They had both proven themselves to be reliable and they were also academically solid students. Shomari continued on as one of the tenth grade reps, but Xolani chose to step down from her role, and the other tenth grade rep position was given to a very promising leader and outstanding student named Jayla. The new ninth grade students to serve as representatives for their grade level were both younger siblings of past BSU students. Siyana was the younger sister of past President Aiyana, and Jaden was the younger brother of Calvin. This was another solid Executive Board and they would be tested to keep the BSU together all year.

We began the school year in the remote setting with no return date in sight. This was very strange to say the least. The difference was that unlike the previous March, the shock value of it was gone. The expectations were that students would be present in class on their Zoom each day. By now the students had been inside their homes and had not spent time with their friends in months. I enjoyed seeing the students I knew who had class with Isaiah. I would step in his room and look at his screen and say hello to the students and the teacher every so often. I held my ASB class via Zoom as well and I spent a lot of time with those students and the BSU students in meetings. In fact, it seemed like I was in meetings all the time. There was ASB class, BSU meetings, Admin meetings, Instructional Cabinet meetings, SLC meetings, faculty meetings, UBSUC meetings, BSU parent meetings, BSU parent planning meetings, BSU's of LA meetings, and Career Speaker Series meetings, and when I was not in a meeting, I was on a phone call, or in a meeting, about one of the other meetings. This was definitely a new normal that we all had to find a way to adapt to until it got better. This is how our BSU adjusted to these changes.

The first thing we did was move our Wednesday meetings to the afternoon at 4:00. School was out at 2:15 and we wanted to give the students time away from the computer, but also have the rest of their day to themselves to do homework or any other activity. We spent a lot of time talking about staying active, and also checking in with each other. Every meeting starting with a mental health check and Denim was great at this. Students still found these meetings as a safe space to express how they were dealing with the pandemic and the meetings sometimes got very emotional. The students were so supportive and encouraging of one another, it was amazing to be present in these meetings. These meetings averaged 70-80 students in the first semester. Another change was multiple board members were given roles during the meetings so that one person would not be doing all the talking. Also, we incorporated fun topics and games like Kahoot in our meetings. We played music while waiting to start meetings. We also incorporated themes into our meetings. For example, the last Wednesday of the month became our Career Speaker Series. This series came as a result of our parent meetings. We found it very powerful when we had Dr. Noelle Reid meet with the group last semester, so in a discussion in one of the parent planning meetings, we decided that we would do this every month. The parents would all go to their networks and invite people to speak to the students. Many names were gathered and a schedule was made with who would be speaking each month. These were evening meetings as well, and this proved to be a great addition to our meetings. The students would hear from people of all walks of life and their stories were very inspirational. The last Tuesday of the month would be our BSU parent meeting. The students were not required to attend these, but it was great to spend time with the parents. To plan those parent meetings, we assembled a small group of parents including Jennifer, Lisa, Mr. Anderson whose son was Gregory, the newly elected Sergeant at Arms on the UBSUC board, Mr. Brinkley, and also Ms. Monroe. In those parent meetings there would often be an invited guest to speak to certain issues the parents were dealing with in helping their children navigate this new normal. Although the students did not attend these meetings, by meeting with their parents it kept the family together by including them in what was going on in BSU. We would invite administrators to the meeting to hear the concerns of the parents. We also invited mental health professionals, college counselors, and financial aid representatives. We played games like Kahoot as well. Since we could not be together physically, we tried to enjoy each other as much as possible virtually.

Early in the semester I began reaching out to schools in the LAUSD that either had, or were looking to start BSU's. In September we had our first meeting in what I called the BSU's of LA Leadership Check-in. My objective was to network with other school BSU's and get more of them to create or stabilize their BSU and also join the UBSUC so their students could enjoy the benefit of attending these conferences and conventions. These meetings would take place on the second Wednesday of each month. My student leaders would join me on these calls initially, but later that would change to me inviting them only when needed. I wanted to limit the time they were on the screen, so we made our first and third Wednesday the primary meeting days. I learned that many schools wanted BSU's, but the reality is that this is a serious time commitment on the job. Most of us have many responsibilities while at school and the time it takes to nurture and grow a BSU requires a lot of time and work, unpaid work. Some schools have the duties split between two or three people, and I think that is a good way to run a BSU as long as the leaders can meet regularly and craft a mission and a vision for the group, and work as a team. The difficulty of this was magnified during the Covid year. Our challenge was we had become this family, and now the inability to get together and enjoy one another was for many students like not being able to see your family. We had to balance seeing each other often on the screen with the physical effects of spending too much time on the screen. I believe we walked that line pretty well because of our outstanding leaders. When we did get together on screen, we truly enjoyed being together.

The ASB students worked very hard to try to bring the school community together using social media. Ms. Monroe was a tremendous resource in this area because she managed the school social media account. She constantly reminded the ASB, BSU, and other student groups to post activities. She helped created social media campaigns that the whole Hamilton community could support. We had a virtual Club Rush early in the year. All the clubs had to create electronic posters and flyers and Club Rush became Rush Week where students had an entire week to visit all the clubs at various times. BSU welcomed new members during our appointed time to be on the screen. We had a virtual Spirit Week where we had dance challenges on social media. Denim created a dance challenge for faculty members, who submitted videos of themselves doing her dance. It was awesome to see. We had students and faculty members send pictures with their pets. The school leaders, including the BSU did all we could to keep the school community together. Denim reached out to the other ethnic club leaders and we held collaborative meetings with our LaSo club and our Desi/ASA clubs just to show support for the other clubs. I thought this was not only a great gesture and show of unity, but it showed Denim's ability to bring people together. My message to the group was that "Covid can change what we can do, but it cannot change who we are." The commitment to scholarship, leadership, and service was still strong within the BSU and probably more on display this year than in any other year. We had to be there for each other in many ways, and we were.

One of the things I decided on my own to do to keep the positive spirit alive was to do random pop-up visits at students' houses. I got the idea while delivering graduation signs to the seniors at the end of last school year. I wanted to see the students and I would hint during our meetings that I would be coming around to see them during the weekends, but I would not say who. Then on Saturday I would choose someone and typically notify the parent of my intentions to surprise the student. These were such great moments, because I truly missed the students and I knew they wanted to see me as well. The visits were only for a few minutes, and we would have masks and keep our distance for the most part, but it felt so good, especially when we would take a picture and send it to the group chat. The students were always wondering who would be next.

The UBSUC Spring Convention had been canceled in March, but by now we were ready to resume with our Fall Conferences for each region. The Southern Region would hold its annual conference in November hosted by California State University Dominguez Hills. This would be our first attempt at hosting a conference or convention completely online. Once again, our students were poised to run for each position on the board. This was to be Denim's redemption year after losing a close race for President in the Southern Regional Conference last fall. Amina was running for First Vice President. Our new tenth grade rep, Jayla was running for Secretary. Madisyn, our Fundraising Chair was running for Treasurer. Cameron was running for Parliamentarian again, and Fisher, who had already been 2nd Vice President decided to run for Sergeant at Arms. By the end of the conference Hamilton would have five students on the Southern Region board. Amina had not been elected to serve as First Vice President, though she would serve in that role in our BSU for both her junior and senior year. All five students would go on to run again for state office in the spring convention which would take place virtually after a year off.

We had decided from the beginning that even if we did not come back to school this year, we would still have a BSU Show, a virtual one that we would stream live for everyone to see. Early on I could not say for sure how we would pull this off, but then again if something like this can be done using technology, the students will find a way.

Shortly after the Thanksgiving Holiday the students approached me with something they had been working on. They said they had a script about how the year 2020 had affected students. They would be casting the show and rehearsing soon. This would obviously be different from our usual shows which usually cast well over 50 students for the show. We discussed the plan to sell tickets and how the show would be streamed. This show would require multiple takes of scenes and Denim would edit the clips until everything was seamless on screen. Just the year before we did our first ever night show for the whole Hamilton community and now, due to a situation beyond our control, we were about to do our first production on screen. I kept thinking to myself, "If we could pull this off that would be amazing." We had to delay the streaming of the show until the beginning of March to make sure the finished product was to our satisfaction. One benefit of Covid was that we were not at school and therefore not pressured to use the auditorium within a specific window of availability. At Hamilton there are productions in our auditorium all the time, so our shows must be done at a specific time so that we are not competing with another production, and since classes have priority over clubs, we have to use the auditorium when we can. This year that wasn't a problem. We wanted to have the show ready while it was still Black History Month, but I didn't think the extra week needed would be a problem, and it wasn't. We were still able to host our Black History Month activities in the virtual space and here is what we did.

One of the highlights of the year for me was actually before February. It was in December when we usually have our BSU alumni meeting. This is where Covid was a benefit for us. I was able to contact BSU alumni going back to 2012 and when we held our meeting there were more than 25 alumni on the call with our current students. It was truly like a family reunion. I was just coming off another zoom meeting so I was a few minutes late. When I logged on to our meeting, I saw faces I had not seen in a long time, but I immediately began to recall special moments at school with our BSU. I jumped right in and began calling out all the alumni who showed up. It was almost too much. I could not stop smiling as I heard the alumni introduce themselves to our current students and share their wisdom as well as their memories. The meeting was special in so many ways, but most importantly it showed the current students the foundation of what they now uphold, and it did so in a way that I could not always do by merely telling them old stories. They got a chance to meet and hear first hand how this BSU, their BSU, has impacted students' lives for years. This was truly one of my best moments in all my years as BSU advisor at Hamilton High School. When we did get to February, we had a similar meeting, but this one was for our Greek Week. Instead of it being a week long we decided to make it a Divine Nine meeting similar to our alumni meeting. We had representatives from most of the fraternities and sororities and after a brief introduction the students were sent to break out rooms to have a more intimate discussion. Though we have several alumni who are now members of those organizations, and many were on the call, it was a different type of meeting, yet still a great time with members of the Black Greek community. Students not only learned about the organizations, but since many were current or former HBCU students, they got additional information about the schools as well. Another way we used social media during this time was when we gave the Hamilton community "28 Days of Black History." Beginning on February 1 each student had to video themselves giving a Black History fact about a person or event. The students had pre-selected days and each day was someone else's turn. It was certainly something to look forward to as it was posted on our BSU Instagram as well as the Hamilton Instagram. Despite the restrictions of Covid we were still able to host Black History Month programs and keep the morale and interest of the BSU. We hosted our own BSU Movie Night where we got together virtually and watched a movie. Students were in their pajamas as they tried hard to simulate a gathering at someone's house. All these activities led to the showing of our BSU Show entitled "Change." This was about a 40-minute show about students who were given an assignment by their teacher to produce a documentary project answering the question, "Did 2020 have a positive or negative influence on your generation?" The main characters Devin and Shantae, played by BSU students Skyler and Samone, respectively, struggle with the assignment at first because everything seemed so negative and only brought their spirits down. They later see that through all the pain there were good things that came out of it all such as the uniting of people from all races against hatred and the mistreatment of one another. The show demonstrated a resilience of humanity to come together in love even when the very act of doing so could be deadly. It showed that people need each other and will find the strength from one another to make it through difficulties that life brings. Ms. Monroe said it best, "It's one thing to do a show. It's another thing when God speaks through you." That is the impact the students had on the Hamilton community and those who needed a positive message in the midst of so much sadness and despair. The show ends with images of people protesting and the students feeling as though they have grown and have a more positive outlook on the future. The dance finale was to Beyonce's song "Mood Forever," and choreographed by Korley. The song was upbeat and positive and you could see that reflected in the dancers as well as how the song itself followed this positive....change. I go back to my wondering whether we could pull this show off this year. The students came through. They not only pulled it off, but they gave a lot of people hope. This was another very proud moment for BSU this year. The momentum of the show carried us to the State Convention where we would get more good news.

The theme of this year's convention was The Black Effect. This virtual convention would include workshops on topics such as financial literacy, Black men in education, and a Divine Nine panel. Five Hamilton students would be running for state board positions and the 2021 BSU of the Year winner would be announced. Since the 2020 convention in the Southern Region was canceled, the adult executive committee decided to let Southern Region host in 2021. When the convention began, I noticed that there were a few more BSU's from the LAUSD present which excited me. It told me that the monthly check-ins sparked some interest in those schools to see what the UBSUC was about. Since we did not have a state convention during the previous year, there was also no current state board. Officers from the various regions worked together to organize and run the convention. When it was time to announce the BSU of the Year, I heard the announcer read off the events and activities of the winner. While she read, I began to smile because I knew she was talking about us. It was an extremely difficult year for BSU's everywhere, I have no doubt, but these amazing students persevered. Their love for one another, their belief in the BSU, and their determination to stay together brought us through the most difficult year imaginable. The reward was the BSU of the Year for the third consecutive time the award was given. A year that began with naming a junior as our President and with me almost leaving the BSU turned into this amazing story. To top it off, all five Hamilton students won their respective races and were named to the state board. There was still work to do, however. We had to award two students with our first ever BSU Legacy Scholarship. I also had to hand out our BSU Awards for Senior Night. I planned to announce all the winners at the same time, but because the Senior Awards Night was virtual, the winners had to be named weeks in advance so everything could be edited. That meant that I could not announce the scholarship winners because we had not decided yet. We would have to wait to announce the winners. I recorded myself reading off the winners of the BSU Awards... "The winner of the BSU Award for Outstanding Scholar goes to Kelli Jones and Jessica Parks. The BSU Award for Outstanding Leadership goes to Janae Burney. The BSU Commitment to Service Award goes to Christiana Nimakoa, Brandon Davis, and Matthew Morales." As you can see it was very difficult to award one winner for each category this year. There was literally a tie for the Outstanding Scholar Award as Kelli and Jessica both had great academic years. The service award went to three people who each played a huge part in helping us get through the year. Christiana crafted letters to send to those who experienced loss throughout the year.

Brandon did an excellent job leading the Scholarship Committee and set an example for those in the committee to step up and lead, and Matthew was one student who was always so encouraging during the BSU meetings. He always had an uplifting message for those who were struggling and showed a lot of emotion in the meetings. All three students were very deserving. The BSU Award of Excellence went to Sierra Shinn and Kaelynn Fayson. These students have been wonderful ambassadors for BSU since they were freshmen. Kelli, Sierra, and Matthew were headed to UCLA, Jessica to UC Davis, Janae was a Posse Scholar headed to Tulane University. Christiana was headed to UC San Diego and Brandon to San Diego State University. Kaelynn, who graduated a semester early, would go on to Cal State University, Northridge. When I put these seniors as well as many others on our website with their college choices, I called them the Class of Resilience. That is what they were. They didn't attend school in person one day their entire senior year but they excelled anyway. They did the work and prepared themselves for college and life after high school in spite of the challenges. I am so proud to say that my son Isaiah was part of this class. I saw him work and put the time in to his studies. He had his best academic year this year. Like so many, he struggled at first, but he found a way. There was one thing left to do and that was to graduate. We found out that the students were allowed to have an in-person graduation at our school site and this was best news ever. Students would get to come together one last time and they could hardly wait. The first part of this was for them to come and turn in all their school belongings such as books and their computer, and then receive their caps and gowns. That day brought much excitement of its own, but the graduation was special. Due to Covid restrictions we divided the class into two separate graduations. I was there for both, the first one as a faculty member, and the second one as a dad. I was so proud to see Isaiah approach the stage, and when his name was called, our Principal, Mrs. Pensamiento signaled for me to come with him. I was already on the stage, so I proudly walked up with him to receive his diploma. Isaiah had not been as involved in BSU as Kenya was. He usually kept to himself, but like many other students who didn't attend many meetings, he was always available when called upon. He carried himself with the respect and class asked of every BSU member and I could not be more proud of him. The day after graduation we presented our two BSU

Legacy Scholarship winners with $500 each. All I had to do was confirm the mailing address with our school financial manager and she would send a check to Janae and to Sierra, who will both forever be known as the first BSU Legacy Scholarship recipients.

This was a truly remarkable year. We finished the year having our first ever returning President, as Denim was unanimously confirmed once again. Whatever anxiety I had when she first became President had long since turned into total confidence. The assumption was that we would be returning to school in the fall, but at that time no one knew for certain. If we did return, we would once again have a strong BSU leadership team in place. It was the end of my eleventh year as BSU advisor. It was my son's graduation year. I had said to myself, and to a few others, that when my son graduates, it would be a time for me to step back and re-evaluate everything. I did know that I would return for another year because I wanted to see those freshmen from the class of 2019 have their turn to lead BSU as seniors. Beyond that year I had not made any commitment, and as of the writing of this book, I am still not certain. There are other opportunities that deserve some serious consideration, and if I do decide to pursue one, I must make sure that my successor is in place and ready to continue leading these amazing students. As I stated when I received the Distinguished Educator Award from my alma mater, "when you are engrossed in the work, rarely do you have time to step back and reflect on the job you've done. You are too busy working." This summer I was hard at work writing this book, and it was a time to reflect on the last eleven years. I finally had a chance to reflect on those early years and how the evolution of this BSU began with a small group of students who didn't want to lose their club. I hope they read this book and I hope they are proud of the role they played in making sure this club existed. It has been a joy to reflect on the stories behind the things we were able to accomplish, and recount for you each class's contribution to making this BSU special. There are high school BSU's all over this country I am sure. However, it was time to tell *this* story about *this* amazing group of young people I have been so blessed to work with. They have had a tremendous impact on Hamilton High School, and they have been influenced by one another to be scholars, to be leaders, and to be servants of humanity. They have become a family on campus, a home away from home, and a true support system for one another. Now that I can reflect, this is what I see.

Epilogue

I did come back for year twelve and the freshman class of 2019 was ready to lead from the first day of school. The Executive Board, the leaders in addition to our President Denim were Amina and Cameron, who served as First Vice President and Second Vice President, respectively. The new Secretary is Chanel, who ran the social media last year. The Treasurer this year is Madisyn and the Financial Secretary is Aliyah, who served as one of the eleventh grade reps last year. The Parliamentarian this year is Bryan, who had a strong desire to serve on the board as he became a positive voice in our meetings while we were away. Fisher served as our Sergeant at Arms again and newcomers Kennedi and Kharli served as Historian and Social Media Coordinator, respectively. Kennedi has been a member of our BSU for four years and is the younger sister of BSU alum Luzine. Kharli is one of the members of our outstanding junior class who now sits on the board. Kharli, like Bryan, became much more involved in BSU during the Covid year where those meetings became such a safe space to share with peers. The BSU Show production team this year started with Jada, who chose Krista and Asenath to join her. Soon after the school year began, however, Asenath transferred to another school. The unanimous choice to fill this role of choreographer on the team was Jazz Moore. Jazz, another senior, was an amazing dancer and longtime BSU and ASB member. I was thrilled to have Jazz on the Executive Board. I had seen how hard she worked in ASB, and I knew that when she was really into a project, she would put everything she had into it, and with dance as her passion, I was excited to see what she could do in this show. The Community Service Committee was led by Olamide, one of the highest-ranking juniors at Hamilton High along with fellow juniors Maleeyah and Jayla. Maleeyah became the new chair of our Scholarship Committee and Jayla, the new Secretary on the UBSUC state board serves as our eleventh grade rep with Shomari. Maleeyah serves as the President of our AMPA Leadership Club and she also served on the Superintendents Student Council. The new chair of the Fundraising Committee is Lauren, who served as eleventh grade rep last year and Dillan is our new Social Activities Committee Chair. Since the UCLA VIPS program has been so important on our campus, and since they require their students to start clubs or have visibility on the high school campus, we created a new position called VIPS Liaison. This position will be held by a member of our BSU who has been selected for the VIPS program. Their job is to inform the BSU what VIPS has to offer and to announce various outreach efforts by UCLA. Our VIPS Liaison this year is Kamal. Another new position we created was the UBSUC Liaison position. This would be a person who is, or has been a member of the Southern Region or state board who has the job of reporting to BSU what events are coming up with the UBSUC.

This board was presented with challenges this year just as with those in the past. First, they have had to get to know a new Principal as Mrs. Pensamiento left to take another position. Our new Principal, Mrs. Baxter has been incredibly supportive of the BSU as she got to know the leaders quite early on. Secondly, the new board also has had to navigate the transition back to school and the trauma that has inflicted within themselves as with their peers. The last time they were at school physically they were in tenth grade. Now they are seniors. For some, that adjustment has been very difficult to manage and as a result we have had an increase in mental health issues.

Third, a new program called the Black Student Achievement Plan has been implemented within many district schools. This program ideally would provide many opportunities and services to black students, which is always appreciated. Since our BSU had many of these types of services in place already, we had to learn to work together and not duplicate our efforts, nor did we want there to be any type of competition between these two groups. BSAP students include all the black students on campus. BSU students are those who have chosen to be a part of this family that we have created. The BSU and the BSAP team have managed this beautifully and we work together on behalf of the students. Lastly, because of some of the transitions going on with the local colleges, we were not able to go on our usual field trips during the first semester, nor were we able to have our annual alumni meeting due to issues of coming onto our campus. We did have our UBSUC virtual Fall Conference again this year hosted by UC Riverside. In that conference new leaders from Hamilton would emerge and become part of the Southern Region Board. Jayla was elected President, Maleeyah was elected First Vice President and Olamide was elected Second Vice President. Siyana was chosen for Secretary, Milan for

Treasurer, and Shomari was elected Parliamentarian. Here we are again. All new candidates, except Jayla. All new winners. Six out of the seven board positions, and we find ourselves again leading the Southern Region. Later during the spring, all six would run for state office. Five would win as Milan lost a close race for Treasurer. With all the changes, the BSU managed to make it through the first semester and came back in January ready for the final semester of high school for the freshman class of 2019. An early highlight of the year was the opportunity for Denim to speak at the CAAASA Roundtable early in the semester. One of her first acts as a BSU member was to come and promote UBSUC at this same event when she was in the tenth grade. Now, a senior, and President of both the UBSUC and Hamilton's BSU, she was on the program. She spoke eloquently and passionately about how her involvement in BSU has impacted her high school career. She finished to a standing ovation from the CAAASA attendees and received praise from California State Superintendent Tony Thurmond who was present remotely. She is the perfect example of resilience after being devastated by losing her bid to become UBSUC President.

The Black History Month activities this year included another Greek Week with the return of the Yard Show. This show featured the return of Derrick Lewis, Hamilton BSU alum and former ASB student who is now attending Cal State Northridge, and new member of Alpha Phi Alpha Fraternity, Inc. Derrick and a few of the Alpha brothers came and gave the students a great show. We also had Mr. Tolson and new faculty member Marcus Davison represent Omega Psi Phi Fraternity, Inc. as well. We hosted Black Arts Week where we had our Jazz on the Quad with our jazz band. We hosted spoken word in the pergola area of the quad which I called the Pergola Café. There had recently been a big fight in that very same area and I wanted the school to know that BSU was not going to let fighting become the norm at school. We wanted to have spoken word and bring people together in the very same place. Then we had our amazing dancers from Ms. Douglas' class present part of the Dance Show on the Quad. All this led up to our annual BSU Show entitled "A Trip to The Past." Jada had already told me that this show would have nothing to do with Covid or the negativity of 2020 and she stayed true to her word. This BSU Show instead took us on a field trip with students from fictional Colin Powell High School.

They were going to visit the African American Museum and specifically the Arts Wing. There they would be shown exhibits covering the last century of Black entertainers. As the students went through each decade, a few realized that when you take pictures of the "statues," they come to life. Our BSU students portrayed stars such as Billie Holiday, Etta James, Aretha Franklin, The Supremes, The Jackson 5, and continued with Michael Jackson, Brandy, TLC, Tupac, and the Notorious B.I.G. The house band once again provided the music and they did a great job as they always do. A former member of our original house band from 2018, Kelsey Kelly, now works at Hamilton with Mr. Tolson, while attending UCLA, another Yankee Bruin. She has contributed her knowledge and experience in several BSU meetings and is constantly there showing her support. This show, like almost all the others, was written and directed by the students themselves. Krista was responsible for the music production and Jazz did the choreography, which had the audience on the edge of their seats every dance routine. The BSU Show was extremely popular on campus and there was once again an evening show for the entire Hamilton community. It was certainly time to take a bow for the hard work that was put into the show.

The last two BSU Shows can be seen on YouTube for all who would like to see them.

In 2011 my first act upon signing on to be the BSU advisor was to put together a show in about a month's time. One of the last activities included in this book was the BSU Show of 2022. As you can see the BSU Show has been a major part of our experience on campus for all the reasons stated in this book. However, we do so much more than put on a show for the school community. The impact of the BSU on the Hamilton community can be seen every day in how the students conduct themselves. It can be seen in how willing the students are to help faculty when something goes wrong. It can be seen in how the older students interact with the underclassmen. This impact can be felt throughout the state of California when we participate in, and help lead conferences and conventions. We have just received our fourth consecutive BSU of the Year Award at the UBSUC State Convention. I am so proud of these students. All of them. From the early days to this very moment. And I hope that my parents, Johnny and Patricia Turner are proud of any role I played in leading this amazing group of young people. So much of what I try to impart to our students comes from the wisdom I received from my parents, the love and the example I received from them. Family is one of my core values. It is always present whenever I work with students. Of course, not all of them need me to be that for them. They have wonderful parents and I love working with those parents to help reinforce those values while their children are under my care. We truly have something special here at Hamilton and you can feel it and see it the moment you step on campus. Now it is time for the freshman class of 2019 to take that next step. Some have already made decisions on where they will be attending college in the fall. Denim will be attending Clark Atlanta University, Amina is headed to Loyola Marymount University, and Cameron to the University of San Francisco. Chanel will be attending UCLA. Madisyn and Krista are headed to Spelman College, and Aaliyah is going to Hampton University. Dillan is going to Cal State Northridge and Bryan will be attending Middlebury College in Vermont. Once again this year we have seniors headed to colleges all across the country including HBCU's, Spelman, Morehouse, Alabama State, North Carolina A&T, Xavier, and Hampton Universities. We have students going to private colleges back east such as Williams College and Syracuse University. California schools represented by our graduates this year include UCLA, CSUN, Sacramento State, UC Riverside, UC Irvine, UC Merced, San Diego State, San Jose State, San Francisco State, and the University of LaVerne. When you include the public out-of-state universities as well as community colleges, at least 60 seniors have committed to college in the fall, and some are still in the process. This is right at the average for our senior class each year. The end of the year is so special and so emotional as our time on campus comes to a close. To my seniors of this year, and to all the BSU students from 2011 to the present, I love you. I thank you for letting me lead you. I thank you for making me a better educator by constantly reminding me what's most important. It will always and forever be about you.

Acknowledgements

To the thousands of BSU students I have worked with these last dozen years, I thank you for belief in, and respect for me as your advisor. Thank you for making the conscious decision to be better scholars, leaders, and servants of humanity. You are the amazing group of young people without whom this book could not be written.

Thank you to Principals Gary Garcia, Brenda Pensamiento, and Jennifer Baxter for you unwavering support, trust, and belief in the work that I was called to do under your watch. I am eternally grateful.

Thank you to the administrators of Hamilton High School who have always been there to not only support, but assist in any way you could so that our BSU could move how we move. Betty Washington, Dan Blank, Stephanie Lartelier, Sean Gosselin, Dr. Mary Reid, Sergio Cota, Henry Lazo, Wesley Ace you guys are the best.

To April Monroe, in every role you have had at Hamilton High School, even now as Assistant Principal, your support, nurturing, guidance, wisdom have meant everything to the BSU. I am truly grateful for our friendship.

To the many Hamilton High School teachers who have supported me and who have given so much to the students to prepare them for their journey, on behalf of the BSU I thank you.

To our amazing counseling staff, past and present, including Karen Sackett, Sherry Bacon, Syd Navas, Megan Melcher, Saul and Alene Plasencia, Robert Harada, Emmely Aquino, Veronica Loera please know you how much you are appreciated by the entire BSU family.

To the Hamilton support staff, Ed Williams, Tony Meniefield, Cedric Johnson, and the Communities in Schools office, Dana Henry, Erin Favre-Smith, Jacqwel Brown, Darnell Sapps you have worked so close with me on behalf of our students. I appreciate all of your support.

To the many parents of all the students I have worked with at Hamilton, I thank you for your trust and your support. It means the world to me that you can leave your students with me having peace of mind that they are cared for.

To the awesome BSU Parent Group, Lisa Shinn, Jennifer Black, Greg Anderson, Chris Brinkley you all were the missing piece we needed to get to that next level.

To Gjenaii Enciso Givhan, thank you for your motivation and your vote of confidence. Your words were my confirmation.

To Starr Thompson, thank you for always supporting the BSU in word and in deed, thank you for helping us establish our brand on campus with our BSU board.

To Keara Williams, you discovered me. Thank you for seeing enough in me to approach me. You started all of this. I hope we have made you proud.

To the colleges and universities, both local and national that have had us on campus, or visited ours, and provided much inspiration to our students. We depend on your guidance and your expertise.

To Nicole Ford, Stepping in The Right Direction has been a blessing to many of our BSU students. Thank you for our friendship and for always looking out for Hamilton's BSU.

To the many guest speakers who have given your time to pour into our students whether in person or via Zoom. You have inspired so many of our students and you have indeed changed lives.

To my distinguished brothers of Alpha Phi Alpha Fraternity, Inc., and particularly Beta Psi Lambda Chapter thank you for inspiring me to go further, do more, and be better.

To the United Black Student Unions of California, the statewide BSU network we have been so fortunate to be a part of. Thank you to the state board and regional boards, advisors, and supporters for all you do on behalf of our students.

To Felecia Turner, your love and support for half my life has been a blessing. Thank you for listening and for contributing so many ideas to our BSU. Thank you for my two favorite BSU students of all time.

Lastly, I want to thank Kenya Turner and Isaiah Turner. You have made, and continue to make, me prouder than you could ever imagine. My favorite thing in life is to be your father. Thank you for being my greatest inspiration.

About the Author

Ken Turner has worked with the youth of Los Angeles for over 35 years. His career has taken him through numerous positions in academia as well as athletics. He served as a youth counselor for the National Youth Sports Program on the campus of USC before taking a position as a teacher's assistant at Horace Mann Junior High (now middle) School. While at Horace Mann, Turner took a position as a volunteer basketball coach which began a 35 year coaching career. He has coached at Dorsey High School, San Pedro High School, St. Bernard High School, West Los Angeles College, Cal State University Northridge, Cal State University Los Angeles, and the Los Angeles Sparks. While at West Los Angeles College Turner started the Ken Turner Basketball Camp with the Westside Extension community outreach program. He coached Dorsey High School to its first ever girl's basketball LA City Championship in 1996 when he was named LA City Coach of the Year. He led West Los Angeles College women's basketball team to its first Western State Conference Championship in 1999 in his first season and was named Western State Conference Coach of the Year. He coached the women's basketball team at

Cal State Northridge to its first ever Big West Conference win in 2001 and he helped lead the Cal State LA women's basketball team to its first appearance in the NCAA Division II tournament 2006. He also served as Athletic Director at Hamilton High School in 2016. Turner credits much of his success as a classroom teacher and mentor to his coaching background.

His career as an educator also began at Horace Mann where he worked as a teacher's assistant, physical education teacher, and English teacher. After being hired as a coach a Dorsey High School, Turner became a special education teacher at Dorsey as well. He has taught at San Pedro High School, and at Hamilton High School where he has spent the last 15 years. In addition to teaching in the classroom Turner has held out of class positions such as Intervention Coordinator and his current roles as Restorative Justice Coordinator and Associated Student Body Sponsor. For the past 12 years Turner has been the faculty advisor to Hamilton's Black Student Union. Under his guidance the BSU has become the largest in the state and was voted the United Black Student Unions of California BSU of the Year for 2018, 2019, 2021, and 2022. He has served as mentor to thousands of students in this role during his tenure at Hamilton. Turner is a member of Alpha Phi Alpha Fraternity, Incorporated. Turner is the proud father of two children, Kenya and Isaiah, and resides in Moreno Valley, CA.